Mornings and Mourning

Mornings and Mourning

A KADDISH JOURNAL

E. M. Broner

HarperSanFrancisco
A Division of HarperCollins*Publishers*

Thanks to:

Kandace Hawkinson, my editor

Steve Hanselman, marketing manager, and Hilary
Vartanian, publicist

Mimi Kusch, production editor, and the production
people

Jaime Robles, text designer

And all the rest of the peppy crew at Harper San
Francisco

An early version of selected portions of *Mornings and Mourning* appeared in the September/October 1994 issue of *Tikkun: A Bimonthly Jewish Critique of Politics, Culture, and Society.*

FIRST EDITION

Library of Congress Cataloging-in-Publication Data
Broner, E. M.
Mornings and mourning : a kaddish journal / E. M. Broner. — 1st ed.
    p.   cm.
ISBN 0–06–061071–9 (cloth: alk. paper)
ISBN 0–06–061072–7 (pbk: alk. paper)
    1. Broner, E. M.—Religion.   2. Women in Judaism.   3. Mourning customs, Jewish.   4. Feminism—Religious aspects—Judaism.   5. Authors, American—Religious life.   I. Title.
    BM729.W8B747   1994
    296.4'45'082—dc20   94–9438
                                                                       CIP

94 95 96 97 98 ❖ HAD 10 9 8 7 6 5 4 3 2 1

This edition is printed on acid-free paper that meets the American National Standards Institute Z39.48 Standard.

To the parting of the curtains

Mornings and Mourning

I am amputated, inconsolable. My father has died.

Now I must invent him, perhaps fictionalize, mythologize him.

Most of all, I will have to find a way to mourn him.

Our first public duty is to announce his death. As a newspaperman he would want his obituary in the press. We will think of him, as it is being composed, with his red pencil, cutting excess and arranging for graceful transitions.

He devoured the newspapers from the "ears," the boxed information above the headline on the front page, to the obits, every edition from the early morning "bluebird" to the evening "owl."

After reading the obituaries, he would say, "Look, somebody wonderful lived."

My father always wanted to be on top of the news, up-to-date. Dates were important to him, beginning with history in grade school. He described his first classes when "I, a young immigrant boy from Russia, developed a crush on Washington and Lincoln."

He was nine, two years into the new language, when he was chosen as poet laureate of Park Street School.

Memory did not fail him, of things trivial or large. The Park Street School cheer was as clear to him in his eighties as at nine.

Stand them on their head
Stand them on their feet
Park Street! Park Street
Can't be beat!

He wrote a poem, then, for Washington's birthday, that began:

Not with fife and not with horn
was George Washington born.

"No fanfare," Dad explained to his children, "Plain-born like me. Anybody can be George Washington." Even a short man with a jutting lower jaw and a red scar across his cheek where, when he was an infant, a kerosene stove had burned him when it had overturned.

As my parents aged, I grew anxious that the data of their lives would be lost. For a year we worked together to write their combined memoir, finishing in time for their fiftieth wedding anniversary. They weren't doing it for themselves, they said, but so the grandchildren would know how it had been in their time. And they called it *All Our Years*.

My mother wrote personally, my father historically.

At their fiftieth anniversary, they sat with their backs to our fireplace, facing family and friends. They opened their red leather-bound memoir. Mother read first. She was dressed in an outfit bought at discount through Cousin Cooky's store: a black slack suit with blue satin cuffs and lapels, the jacket strewn with a pattern of blue roses.

Mother began:

I was the youngest of six children. My first recollection of poverty was that eight of us lived in a three-room little house with an outside privy. It did not have any floors. The only toy I had was a doll made out of rags.

For breakfast, we would have boiled water with milk and bread; for lunch we had soup made out of boiled water, a little goose fat, squeezed-in fresh garlic, a little salt, and we would break in a couple of pieces of dry bread. For supper, we would each have a piece of herring, with a boiled or baked potato, a glass of tea, and a piece of bread.

My father smiled proudly, listening to his wife's literary effort. For the occasion he wore a navy jacket, white boutonniere, and a matching navy tie decorated with red and gold antique cars.

In his section, my father was part of an epoch:

My lifetime has spanned nearly three-quarters of the twentieth century. When I was born in the town of Polonye, in the Ukraine, right in the thick of the Pale [where] five million Jews lived . . . England was engaged in fighting the Boer War. The British Empire was at the height of its influence. . . . France was just recovering from the Dreyfus case which had split the nation. . . . President McKinley had just been assassinated in Buffalo by a crazed anarchist. . . . Germany was flexing its muscles. . . .

In Russia, the Procurator General had proclaimed his policy toward the Jews: one-third would convert, one-third would emigrate. And one-third would be allowed to remain and starve.

(*All Our Years*, by Paul Masserman and Beatrice Weckstein Masserman, unpublished manuscript)

History stayed with him.

As a freshman in college, I returned from a history exam with the short-answer test in my hand.

"Test me," said my dad, smiling in anticipation.

Out of a hundred questions, he scored ninety-eight.

"That was European history," he apologized, "and I'm a bit rusty. I would have scored better on American."

∾

Leisure World

In 1979 my parents moved from the cold Detroit winters to balmy southern California. They settled into the retirement community of Leisure World.

When Dad saw the sign at the gates, he balked.

"Work is the meaning of life," he said, "not leisure."

When I visited him there, even in the last two years of his life, Dad would test my memory on recent history.

He might ask, "May 1985? What happened?"

I would usually not remember.

"Reagan visits the cemetery at Bitburg, Germany, the site of the graves of the S.S."

"Why?"

"To shore up German chancellor Helmut Kohl with his right wing."

"May they all be under the tombstones," says my mother.

"Here's another for you," says my father. "Also May, also '85."

"Tell me."

"The press could tell you," says my father. "There was a TWA hijacking by the Hezbollah, the separation of Jews from non-Jews, and the passengers held captive for seventeen days."

"May the Hezbollah come down with cholera," says my mother.

"October '85." Dad is on a roll.

"What was it?"

"The *Achille Lauro*, the Italian liner, is hijacked by Arabs, and the body of Leon Klinghoffer, in his wheelchair, is thrown over the railing."

"May they drink dirty water and get typhoid," says my mother.

"February '85?"

I am weary of being uninformed. I keep silent as Dad plunges ahead.

"Natan Sharansky freed from the Gulag. The next month? March '85?"

He doesn't wait for me to pretend to remember.

"Kurt Waldheim, former director of the United Nations, accused of hiding his Nazi past and of being an officer that sent the Greek Jews to Mauthausen."

Mother choruses, "Until the tenth generation may Waldheims be cursed."

"Try another year, Dad," I suggest. It's embarrassing to get none right.

"Here's an easy one: September 6, 1986?"

Blank.

"Two Arabs kill twenty-one in an Istanbul synagogue with machine guns and hand grenades."

"Daddy," I say, "that's all just about Jews. Other things happened. Reagan was elected to a second term. Gorbachev leads the Soviet Union. That was the year the spaceship *Challenger* exploded with all those astronauts."

"That's true," Dad acknowledges.

"And Marcos left the Philippines. And Duvalier left Haiti, and in the Soviet Union there was the meltdown at Chernobyl."

Dad says, "That's also news."

"You take your news and I'll take mine," says my mother to me.

The one date, however, that you can now and forever quiz me on is Thursday, January 15, 1987, when this history begins.

New York, Sunday, January 25, 1987

"Whu wha." "Whu wha." I think I hear over the phone a child asking for water.

It's "Whu ya wan?" The voice on the phone is so abrupt I almost drop the receiver.

"What time is the morning service?" I ask.

"Seven forty-five," says the sexton and cuts himself off as he hangs up.

He is the shammes of a synagogue I will call *Beit Hatikva,* House of Hope.

This is not my first phone call on the matter.

I phone various synagogues in the neighborhood about attending regular services. After all, my father asked for a daily kaddish, the prayer for the dead.

It is not the custom for morning and evening services to be held daily at the Conservative and Reform branches of Judaism, at least those within traveling distance. I go through "synagogue" in the Yellow Pages, from "Brotherhood" to "Garment Center" to "Wall St. Synagogue." One had a name that began with "Young."

Young, I think. That might be a youthful congregation and they're nearby. I phone.

"Do you have daily services?"

"For what purpose, may I ask?" The secretary does not sound youthful.

"For me," I say, "to mourn for my father."

"Oh no," says the secretary. "We do not allow our women to mourn."

I picture their women with brimming eyes and fixed smiles.

"But what if they're in mourning?"

"There are professional mourners," she tells me, "for just such a purpose. You hire them."

"No, it's for me to do," I tell her.

"Not with us it isn't," she says. "Also, a warning. You'll have a hard time getting an Amen." She pronounces it in Hebrew, "Ah-main."

The second mystery of the day in the lexicon of worship.

The secretary was right.

I would learn that, from certain quarters, when I rose to speak the Mourners' Prayer, there would be a silence at each of the four or five places where the congregation was required to say Amen. The prayer was, therefore, regarded as null and void, my father dishonored.

New York, Monday, January 26

I set the alarm for 6:30 to wake up and exercise. No way for me to tumble into hard-learned Hebrew without being fully awake.

I appear at my neighborhood synagogue at 7:45, the workforce of the city already pouring out of the PATH trains from New Jersey and out of the Lexington and Broadway–Seventh Avenue lines.

The shopkeepers have swept or hosed down their walks. The news vendors have spread out their wares at dawn. So it is no surprise that the doors of the synagogue are unlocked.

I enter to find a small davening room, a prayer room, on the street level. Only one person is sitting there, a gaunt, gray-haired woman. She sits behind a clothes rack on wheels with a curtain stretched across it. I smile uncertainly and sit across the aisle from her.

"Here! Here!" she points to her bench. "They make us sit here, behind the *schmata*. That shit Schlomo said it was too see-through and put a tallis over the rack. I didn't know whether the ark was opened or closed. I don't know if it's summer or winter.

"Damn 'em to hell," says Doris, "especially Schlomo and that miserable Ornstein and that weird Joshua."

She's giving me the characters, but what's the plot?

Although it's before 8 A.M., I detect alcohol on Doris's breath as she rages. In her hand, Doris is clutching a much-folded transliteration of the kaddish.

"I rush in only to say kaddish for my sister and rush back out again. I wait in the corridor. I won't sit behind the *schmata* any longer. Let 'em all burn in hell."

I see Doris at morning davening only once more because she is finishing her kaddish time. What I don't know is that soon I'll be talking just like Doris.

These are new words in my life, *davening* and *kaddish*. Jewish fathers say, on the birth of a son, "Here's my kaddish."

I have brothers who will honor their father in the Midwest and on the West Coast, but I am the oldest, a woman, a daughter determined to be my father's kaddish.

Until now, I have remained seated during the Mourners' Prayer. I have lost no one close, not parent, husband, or sibling. I have been passive in this world of mourning.

According to custom, it will be eleven months, minus one day, seven days a week, and I will be standing and uttering the kaddish for my father. I will be a davener, a noun usually referring to a man who prays with daily ardor. And I will never totally know why I'm doing this or why I chose this particular and demanding synagogue to house my grief.

Leisure World, Friday, January 16

We arrive in Leisure World, in Laguna Hills, California, our suitcases carrying the same clothing, still unpacked from our visit here this past week. We flew from LAX to JFK Thursday, received the phone call midnight our time, 9 P.M. California time, and turned around and flew back to California today.

BEFORE THE PHONE CALL

On my last visit to my father, it had been a slightly overcast January day in southern California. Still we convinced Dad to take us to the pool.

On our walk to Club House Four, I talked to him and he did not reply. He was now wearing a double hearing aid. Sometimes Dad became vague. I was worried.

"Dad," I asked, testing both hearing aid and concentration, "what are President Reagan's motives in his actions?"

"Blood lust," said my father. Then twinkling, "So, do I pass the test?"

That afternoon, to warm his body, he lowered himself gingerly into the jacuzzi. He was supposed to be in there only five minutes, a time limit for the elderly, but he stayed until his skin crinkled. He was interviewing the jacuzzi sitters—the women wearing bathing caps trimmed with rubber petals, the men dipping into the hot water or out on the ledge to cool.

Suddenly the jacuzzi was invaded by a husky fellow with a bristling mustache. He monologued; he interrupted; and finally he departed, splashing water out of the jacuzzi.

My dad looked up after him,

"Those sixties," said my dad. "They get away with everything."

But the hot swirling water did not relieve the chill. At night his breathing was labored and he caught a slight flu. He was uncomfortable all the night.

Mother would ask, each time Dad rose, "Honey, what can I do for you?"

In the morning, after a night of his nausea and diarrhea, Mother asked, "Honey, how are you feeling now?"

"Not so good," said my dad, one of the few complaints I ever heard him make about his health. It seemed to be a mild enough flu, so Bob and I rose in the morning, fretted about whether to remain, but decided to fly back to New York on our special rate rather than lose our fare.

A pile of mail awaited us in the city. One envelope I left for last, a large white mailer that looked as if it contained an announcement for the new winter line at Macy's. But it was from the National Endowment for the Arts. I had been awarded twenty thousand dollars for a novel-in-progress.

I phoned Leisure World and spoke to my mother.

"How is Dad?"

"We're dressing him to take to the doctor."

She and my brother Jay were pulling the jacket up over listless arms.

"I hope it's nothing," I said, worried, "but I have good news," and I told her.

Mom called, "Paul, the U.S. government honored your daughter and gave her a lot of money."

I heard his voice from the bedroom, "Wonderful! Wonderful! That makes me feel better already."

Soon after, he died.

Legends began forming around my father. There had been no sickness. It was too abrupt and unacceptable.

"God kissed him on the cheek just like He did to Moses," said my mother. "Dad was *ausgehapt,* grabbed up."

And I would be grabbed up in a different life, entering a new kind of community, all to please my father.

And I would learn of the four phases of grieving:

Aninut, the wailing time, from death until burial.

Shivah, sitting in grief at the designated place of mourning, for a period of a week or less.

Schlosshim, the thirty days after the death when no outside entertainment is allowed the mourner.

Kaddish, the eleven months from the time of the death. A noun of multiple meanings, kaddish refers to the Mourners' Prayer, to the months during which one mourns, and to the one taking on the responsibility for the public grieving.

For dying is no small matter.

New York, Tuesday, January 27

I enter the small prayer room used in the early mornings. With Doris gone, I am the only woman in the room, and, with one or two exceptions, I will remain so for the next eleven months.

I look around. I will soon learn who will be my cohorts and who my enemies.

One ancient is davening. They are all ancients. The shammes, or sexton, addressed by his occupation, is ninety-five. He has a competitor in Rodney, at ninety-seven. Although the shammes dresses for the job, Rodney takes out his uncomfortable teeth and lisps his prayers, shuffles in slippers, eases open the buttons of his shirt so he can flap in the room.

Rodney's job is to pass around the charity box. There he sits on the bench guarding the *pushke*, the silver container for charity, and, in the overheated small room, dozes. I learn that he has dozed too long, all alone one morning this past month, and the silver *pushke* is stolen. Even though falling asleep on the job, Rodney covets the shammes's position.

The shammes counts the crowd. He counts in the Hasidic way, "Not one, not two, not three."

I learn that if one is counted, perhaps the evil eye up there can also count you.

"We got not seven," says Fred, who will turn out to be the joker of the crowd.

The shammes comes to "not eight," including himself. Without a minyan, the required ten, one cannot read the most sacred prayers during the service: the kaddish, the prayer for the dead; the barkhu, the prayer of praising the Almighty; and the keddusha, the prayer chanted while standing that includes "Holy, Holy, Holy."

So the shammes goes out into the street hunting for Jewish men. No matter how hard-pressed he is to get up the ten, I am not counted in the crowd. I am not "not one."

"Here comes half-a-man," the shammes chuckles when he greets me today and every day. "Too bad. I need a whole."

He now returns with his find, a street cuckoo, but Jewish. This bird hoots and crows throughout the prayers. It's Tsibble, Onion, as they call him, a garment worker from Williamsburg who trains in for the kaddish. I start and stare whenever the ninth man lets out a whistle.

"Not nine!" says the shammes.

The shammes asks, "Tsibble, did you get a seat on the subway?"

Tsibble whistles and nods.

"Know how he gets a seat?" the shammes asks. "He eats onions and garlic, and soon he has the whole car to himself! Isn't that right, Tsibble?"

Tsibble whistles and hoots his way around the room like a modern-day Harpo Marx and soon discovers me behind the curtain.

I'm surprised to hear him speak.

"Hello, Miss," he says. "Miss, once Jew ate onion and garlic. Nobody come near us. They hold the nose." Tsibble holds his nose. "Now Jew don't eat onion. Jew don't eat so much garlic. Jew smell so sweet." Tsibble sniffs his armpits. "And still no minyan."

The men, especially one young serious man named Ralph, laugh, and Tsibble is emboldened to continue.

"Once we had benches, so dirty, rough nails would stick you in your *tuchas.*" Tsibble grabs the seat of his pants and leaps up. "Now the benches so nice, beautiful, smooth, no nails, also no minyan."

Arnold, a sports fan, looks out the high window of our little room, watching for the rabbi.

"The rabbi's getting ready to park! A minyan at last! No, someone has his parking space. He could circle around until Shavuoth and miss the opening play."

We wait minutes more while the rabbi circles the block.

The shammes says, "Here he comes! The *ganze megilla!* The whole story. The real McCoy. The tenth man!"

The rabbi enters, rubbing his hands together.

"Good morning, gentlemen."

He sees me and looks puzzled.

"Start the blessings, then, speedily, we'll get to the Mourners' Prayer, all in a half-hour, tops. We'll do everything like in the express lane at the checkout counter, rung up, bagged, and on your way."

The rabbi approaches me.

"Miss, may I ask who you're here for?"

I say, "My father."

He acknowledges the black ribbon of mourning above my heart.

"You're still in *schlosshim,* the first month of mourning?"

I say, "Yes."

"Fresh wound," says the rabbi. "Your father's lucky to have such a daughter."

The others are getting impatient.

One yells, "Get the show on the road!"

"On the other hand," the rabbi lowers his voice, "you haven't brothers who can say the kaddish?"

"No," I lie.

One of a frowning group overhears us and says, "It doesn't count that way."

But Fred leans over and says, "Remember the two sisters used to come say kaddish for their father?"

"Rain or shine," says the shammes, "the whole time. Nice girls."

Fred laughs, "'Nice girls, in their seventies."

There is a group huddled together.

One dark, bearded fellow insists, "I never saw women here."

"It was before your time with us, Rabbi Ornstein," says the rabbi of the synagogue.

Then Fred asks, "Rabbi, what happened to our five-items-or-less express lane?"

The rabbi says, "Right now, Fred. All rise. This will be the Broadway–Seventh Avenue Express, Forty-second Street nonstop to Seventy-second, then directly on to Ninety-sixth. Hold onto your hats."

"What page?" I ask.

"It's starting already," says Rabbi Ornstein.

Another of this group, a pudgy person with a youthful face and a white beard, also complains, "If it's not the page, next she'll want the place on the page."

Out of the corner of his mouth, the shammes says, "Page seventeen."

A voice pipes up. A slender young man, almost hidden behind the puffy figure with the white beard, says, "It should be stopped before it begins."

There appears to be at least a trio of objectors, perhaps Doris's crowd of Ornstein, Schlomo, and Joshua.

I hear Joshua's name called. I am more concentrated on his rainbow prayer shawl and embroidered yarmulke than on this young man himself.

Who is he, so flamboyant among dour Ornstein and bushy Schlomo? He may be, like Schlomo, a *baal tshuv*, a prodigal son who has returned to the fold, filled with zeal. The problem is, he may have turned into a zealot. Or is he a convert, therefore doubly observant? And what of his background, race or races not usually in attendance in the synagogue? He is deeply self-conscious. Something is unsettled amid the finery.

The beginning blessings are read in a cadence so fast I can't keep up in English, much less labor the Hebrew, in which the congregation gives thanks for the One:

"Who has given us understanding to distinguish between day and night."

The congregation repeats the last four words, *"Behn yom v'lilah."*

The rabbi says, ". . . Who has not made me a heathen."

"Nechri." Heathen.

The rabbi says, ". . . Who has not made me a slave."

"Avod," says the congregation.

The rabbi says, ". . . Who has not made me a woman."

"Esha."

"What?" I exclaim.

Tsibble giggles, "Who has made me a *schlemazl.*"

And there is the curtain, that ugly curtain over the women's bench. "The *schmata,*" as Doris called it.

I go home and say to Bob, "I can't do it."

"That's all right with me," says Bob.

"Dad will surely understand," I say.

"Surely," says Bob.

But I go back. And the next day too. My life begins to simplify around the shul; Bob's life is full of appointments and work as well as the ordinary chores of life. Tomorrow he goes to the dentist. His filling has fallen out. Then, in the evening, artist friends come to the loft to see his new work.

On Thursday he will call Bob Blackburn, whom he has known for thirty years. Blackburn organized the long-lasting Printmaking Workshop, where Bob now has a grant to work as artist-in-residence. In preparation, he is doing drawings for etchings and monoprints.

My days are quiet, the only sound coming from my studio, the soft click of the computer as it tries to thread together the many characters of my novel. I take this crowd with me to the West Village where I have a small office in the Writers' Room, an urban writing colony.

Even though I also work in my loft, I need to be able to lock my door and walk to business. This big cast needs its own space to sing alto, tenor, bass, and soprano. That kind of internal music has to be where there is no other noise.

New York, Friday, January 16

As we gather our bags for the return flight, never having unpacked them from the day before, I add my zip-up bag with a manila envelope containing artifacts from my father's life.

THE PHOTOGRAPHS

Dad and Mom in Leisure World are in constant sunlight since they moved to the Southwest. My dad always wears short-sleeved shirts. In one photo, Dad is smiling in his canary yellow shirt, his glasses slipping down on his nose. In the shuffling of snapshots, there is Dad in a short-sleeved white shirt, head bowed in Sabbath prayer, the candles at Mom's side gleaming.

There is another, the three of us in my parents' courtyard. I, who am five-foot-four, stand between my mother and father, they shoulder-high to me. Their white hair catches the late afternoon light.

I pack photos of celebration from Dad's eighty-fifth birthday. Our cousins, who emigrated from Russia ten years ago, are grinning at him. They are stocky women, three sisters, older and younger than my mother. They are Polya, Bronya, and Esther. Polya's son, Valery, has driven them down from Hollywood, a city whose inhabitants have added Russian to their vocabulary.

Dad dressed for the occasion in his favorite patriotic outfit, a cherry red shirt and blue-and-white striped pants. He blows out the candles of his cake, surrounded by his youngest grandchildren, eight, four, and two, puckering up their lips to help him extinguish that galaxy of light. His older grandchildren, in their thirties, swing their young cousins by the hands, walk them upside down, the soft baby palms of the small children padding on the carpet.

Dad was worried about Leisure World when they moved eight years ago from the Midwest. He could barely help Mother pack to leave the brutal winters, the icy streets where she was afraid to walk outside. He was afraid he wouldn't find enough work to keep him busy.

Soon enough he found work aplenty, editing his synagogue bulletin, joining various organizations, and being proudly the oldest alum, 1925, of the University of Michigan Leisure World Association.

"How do you do it, Dad?" I asked.

"A newspaperman always has his tools with him," he told me. "Curiosity, a sharpened pencil, and his mouth."

I have also packed a framed photo taken in 1972, fifteen years earlier. It's one of those tourist photos snapped at the Western Wall in Jerusalem. The stone of the *Kotel* is rough-hewn. The sky is overcast. My dad is davening, the phylactery on his head, pushing back his summer straw hat. Next to him, but encapsulated in his own thoughts, is Bob. Bob's hair is long, as was the style then, worn over his ears, covering his neck, blown by the Jerusalem wind over his eyes. He is touching the warm stones of the *Kotel*, transmitting messages to three of our children back in the States.

We have spent most of the year on sabbatical in Israel, and my parents are visiting.

My dad has just retired at seventy-one from a public relations job. He retired late, too late to dream. As he walked around Jerusalem he became aware that all around him people had extravagant, impossible, fantastical dreams.

"I met a man in the *schvitz*, the bathhouse, who is planning to start a university, and he's going to name it after himself," my dad announced.

Another day, "I met someone starting a newspaper. Now that could interest me."

A third time, "I met an old geezer who is learning Hebrew and plans to go to a development town to teach them English."

Although in Jerusalem age did not seem to prevent a new life—political, literary, or social—it seems to me that Dad, in the last half of his life, did everything a bit late.

ℵ

New York, Wednesday, January 28

One of the curiosities of *Beit Hatikva* is Tsibble, the wise fool of the group. Ralph, a thirtyish, regular member of the minyan, who finished his eleven months of kaddish and now attends the services out of need and habit, begins to smile as soon as Tsibble enters the room wearing a cloth cap and mismatched pants and jacket.

"I don't understand Yiddish," says Ralph, "but he was the only one who made me smile my year of mourning."

Tsibble heads for the lace curtain on the women's side. It is the kind of curtain one would have seen in a

1930s living room or parlor, only this is stretched across a clothes rack that I push away from me when I seat myself on my bench.

Ralph laughs, seeing Tsibble play peekaboo with me.

"Get away from there, Tsibble," says the bulky congregant with the short white beard, whom I now know is Schlomo.

"And you, lovely lady," he continues, "get behind the curtain. We can't look at you during prayers."

"Show modesty," says Joshua, in his sartorial splendor, the matching yarmulke and tallis.

Doris must have been a "lovely lady" also.

Schlomo marches to the women's bench and pushes the clothes rack across my instep.

"You dazzle us," he says.

I wonder if I'm dazzling the others when the shammes says, "Don't bother her. She's not bothering you."

The shammes is to prove my ally in the months of daily services. He shuffles over to cue me on the page. He is my mentor and my taskmaster.

He taps the page impatiently. "Say it. Say it so God can hear it or your father won't get up there." He points up to heaven, a locale with which he's daily more familiar.

"Don't let the old man bother you," says Fred, a salesman, also the group prankster, jester, joker. "He's impatient. He's not got much time left."

Fred tells a joke a day. His jokes are often God jokes or Miami Beach jokes. Sometimes God appears at Miami Beach. The first joke I hear him tell is a God joke:

> A religious old coot places all power in the hands of the Lord. A great flood comes to his town, and

tures of these shell-covered creatures with torsolike bodies.

Jay feels like a grandson toward our parents, for he is younger than I. Mother bore Jay when she was forty-three and Dad about forty-seven. Jay will talk about this on the Sunday afternoon of the funeral. He will speak of how he joined the football Little League and learned with all the Little Leaguers how to tackle.

The fathers stood tall before their nine-year-olds, awaiting their assault. Jay would rush to tackle Dad, who then was fifty-four and five feet tall. Dad would go sprawling on the ground, his glasses flying. Then he would right himself, dust the bits of grass from his pants, search for his thick glasses, and await another attack.

My dad wasn't that way when I was little. Girls don't attack their fathers; girls don't hurl themselves with energy across the field.

Our companionship was at the Parkman branch library, a cathedrallike building with flying buttresses, stone walls—all this elegance and free reading in Detroit. In my childhood the Parkman branch had a good foreign section: Yiddish, Hebrew, Polish, Greek, German, and other languages read by its immigrant borrowers. Every Friday my dad would borrow seven books, one for each day, and would return them, all read, on the following Friday. To follow his example, I would take out seven of the slimmest books, usually from the poetry or theater section, so I, too, could return them read.

I don't know how my father jammed so much information into himself, pages of Judaica, sociology, memoirs, and political history.

He was always taking civil service tests, applying for a better, more secure position, yet when he arrived for the interview, having been selected for his high scores, he would be dismissed as a smart shrimp who could not possibly assume authority.

Dad was self-conscious about his appearance. When my middle brother, Monte, was born, my father worried that his son would be short and would also inherit Dad's jutting lower jaw. For years my brother went to orthopedists to be measured. For years he went to orthodontists to have his braces adjusted. My brother Monte is a fine height and has a perfect bite. But, though all of us children easily topped our dad in height and were more perfect in bite, we did not exceed him in intelligence.

New York, January

One day the rabbi calls me in. He has to fill out his three-by-five card on me, beginning with the date of my father's death.

"How old was he?" he asks.

"Eighty-six," I say.

"These days, that's not so old," the rabbi tells me. "The whole board of trustees is in its seventies. You're not even allowed to study Kabbalah until you're forty. You only reach your stride in your seventies. My father was eighty and living so nicely, and then he went. It's never the right time."

"How do we let go?" I ask him.

"Sometimes *they* let go. And in some way *HaMalach HaMovis*, the Angel of Death, warns them that he's coming."

"I think of how much he was doing and how little others are doing—" I begin, but the rabbi cuts me off.

"You can't choose a stand-in when the Street Cleaner comes."

"Street Cleaner?"

"Also known as the Rag Man," says the rabbi. "But let's get down to business. By the Hebrew calendar, your kaddish will be ended in the month of *Tevet*. By the regular calendar that figures out to December 4."

"Don't finish with him so fast," I say.

"I'm only a bookkeeper for the Almighty," he tells me. "Now let's go in. And don't fight me over the curtain. The curtain isn't the issue. Your father is the issue."

But the curtain *is* an issue.

The shammes is annoyed that we're entering late.

He spends the next forty-five minutes either calling out the page for me or rushing over to me. For some reason, I am neither nervous nor offended by him. Let him yell a little.

After prayers, there is the *kiddish,* the after-service munchies.

"Shammes," says Arnold, "don't break your leg rushing to the herring."

Arnold sits in the little room by himself reading the sports pages of the various newspapers. He has discarded the front sections.

Fred and Larry invite me to join them.

"Join us for schnapps," says Larry the button man. "It'll open your eyes."

Fred says, "Give yourself a lift. Give the day a push-up."

I am packing up my briefcase as the shammes shuffles quickly to the room near the kitchen. The shammes even uses his elbow to hurry his way out. Then he stops and turns to me.

"There are three things," he says, "that old men love: davening, herring, and schnapps."

He takes another step forward, then pauses again.
"Maybe four. Sex."

"Sex?" I ask.

"Sure, lady," says the shammes. "Stick around."

He swings his cane jauntily, clearing the way to the *kiddish* room.

My father told me something quite different about his neighbors at Leisure World.

"There are two things old people like," said Dad, "schnapps and talking. At the supermarket they buy a widow or widower's portion of food but a half gallon of liquor. And talking, that's their legacy."

I catch up with the shammes. I am courtly with him. I worry lest he stumble, lest he put his weight on the cane before he's ready to descend the stairs.

If I hold onto his elbow, will I save him?

With more attention, could I have saved my father?

Leisure World, Week of January 16

My father had told me that, when he was a nine-year-old immigrant from Russia, all of Milwaukee collaborated in saving him.

In their attached house in Leisure World, I take the bound memoir my parents coauthored and reread it. I linger over Dad's description of becoming an American.

This involved going to public school, Hebrew school, and once to the library:

> We were in this country only a month or so when our teacher took us to the library, introduced us to the librarian, showed us how to sign out books and

take out a library card, and even picked out books for us. I told the librarian I wanted a small book with a lot of pictures. She gave me a book by Audubon on birds of America. I was uninterested, but I took the book and returned it a few days later. . . . I forgot the library.

The teacher started telling us about Washington, Jefferson, and, above all, Lincoln, and I was fascinated.

In the fall, a girl who lived in the same four-flat with us told me that the librarian wanted to see me. We loved and respected our teachers and all others who had anything to do with school and learning. So the next day I rushed to the library. The librarian greeted me warmly and then asked me why I hadn't been to the library since the first visit. I told her I didn't like the book picked out for me.

She asked what I liked. When I told her I didn't know, she went and picked out several books, including two fairy tale books and one about American history. That is how I became a bookworm, and my teachers were to call me General, "General Information."

During the week of *shivah*, in their Leisure World attached house, my mother and I talk about Dad's love for books.

I look at the last library book withdrawn by my father. It still has the bookmark. I think of how he read a book nonstop, and as his eyesight worsened his head would bend until his nose almost touched the page. Like reading the words and sniffing the paper at the same time.

"This is only the second overdue notice in his life," says my mother.

"What was the first?" I ask.

"He had only a few author's copies of the book he coauthored, *The Jews Come to America,* and he was running low, so he borrowed one from the library and never returned it. He would hide the notices: 'Mr. Paul Masserman, Please return the book *The Jews Come to America,* by Masserman and Baker.' Finally they stopped sending them."

I touch his book in the bookcase.

"I have two," said Mama. "Take one. Take any book you want."

"No. You're still here," I say.

"Who knows for how long?"

"Forget it, Mom," I say. "You're not going anywhere."

"Remember how your father saved the libraries in Milwaukee?" says Mother.

Some years ago, I was invited to Milwaukee by the Friends of the Library. The librarians were desperate. The state legislature had withheld funding, and the free library system was in danger of closing. I publicly read my father's tribute to the Milwaukee Public Library that had made him a bookworm. The city's newspapers sent reporters to the meeting, and the *Milwaukee Sentinel* quoted from my father's memoir.

In just days, the legislature voted to fund the public libraries.

New York, Thursday, January 29

After early morning prayers I rush to take the subway to Forty-second, the shuttle to Grand Central, and the North White Plains train to the stone buildings and green hills of the Westchester college where I teach. I'm in the world of manors and students to the manor born.

I have left behind the dirty main street on which the sixty-year-old synagogue is located, in a section of town where few Jews live. I have left behind about ten homeless on each block, sleeping in doorways, beseeching at subway entrances, hands out for a bun near the Superette.

I have left behind the gagging odor of garbage and ammonia from urine.

The winter term has begun. I missed the first class Tuesday, January 20, sitting *shivah* in California.

I missed the meeting of the Women's Committee of PEN.

I missed a book party at the Center for Inter-American Relations on Park Avenue.

I missed a late afternoon art viewing at a friend's studio and a luncheon with a former student who is now a college professor.

I had not even looked at my calendar. I was in the past until I returned to the city on Friday, January 24.

At the college I am teaching a workshop called "The Stretch of Fiction." We are reading books realistic and surrealistic. We are reading serial novels for my students who have a hard time conceiving beyond the story.

We will read:

Stones for Ibarra, by Harriet Doerr, about strangers in a strange land, Americans working and dying in Mexico.

My students will enjoy the author's bio, the fact that she completed her B.A. at Stanford fifty years after she began at Smith, and that she wrote the book in her writing class. My students will secretly pose for book photos and feel they have all the time in the world.

Country of the Pointed Firs, by Sarah Orne Jewett, a nineteenth-century collection of stories set in a fishing village in Maine. My students will say, "This is a yawn," perhaps not enjoying these pristine stories. The student writers are on a career track. What do Maine, a fishing village, and the characters of that town have to do with them?

The Woman Warrior, by Maxine Hong Kingston, about growing up as a Chinese American daughter. I believe my women will become mythic in their writing. Dragons will appear. Ghosts will haunt their tales.

The House of the Spirits, by Isabel Allende, a political, fabulist novel about the coup in Chile. I bet my students will begin papering their assignments with butterflies and have the dead past rise from their cemeteries, solemnly observing the present characters.

I am debating about other books, like those dealing with the romance of the family, the tragedy of family. My students are hormonal. Their stories are about affairs, casual or intense, hetero- or same-sex, but, all in all, their deeper interest is the family.

I think of Dennis McFarland's *The Piano Room,* the story of two brothers, one of whom has died before the book begins. There is also the praised blue-collar tragedy, Russell Banks's *Continental Drift,* and the recent serial novel, *The Elizabeth Stories,* by Isabel Huggan. In *The Elizabeth Stories* a girl grows from childhood through high school, learning the bitter truths of insufficient parenting and sexual violence. There is also Alice Hoffman and her magical fiction set in the suburbs. Or Carole Maso's *Ghost Dance,* on madness and separation and continuation in the family.

I am so excited working out the calendar to be photocopied for the semester that, for a moment, I believe my students cannot help but love each and every book.

But then I remember, also, that students can resist anything or anyone assigned.

Last semester I announced the date for the reading by an award-winning writer. This is an assignment, I said sternly. The chairs were set up in the reading room. The writer arrived, but few of the writing students attended.

I teach in both the privileged East and the underprivileged Midwest. In the East a student leans leisurely against the doorjamb of my office and makes an announcement, calling me by my first name. High tuition gives one the privilege of egalitarianism.

"Esther, I have decided to go for greatness."

In the Midwest at the state university, I speak to two of my talented playwrights, one a telephone installer, the other a clerk.

"I will fly in one more time to deliver my final grades," I inform them. "Be in my office at this same hour, and we will work on getting you scholarships for graduate school."

"Yes, Professor Broner," each assures me.

Neither shows up. They have not given themselves permission to go for greatness.

I have risen to the rank of professor in the English department in the Midwest. I am a visiting writer in the East.

In the synagogue, I have no rank or position.

New York, Friday, January 30

Tsibble is pushing the curtain back and forth on its rack and wiggling his fingers at me. "Hello, lady!"

Says pudgy Schlomo, "Tell that nutbread Tsibble he's in the wrong pew."

Fred tells Schlomo, "You go through the pogrom of pogroms like he did, you'd be in the wrong pew too."

"Shammes," says sour Rabbi Ornstein, "how long we gotta wait?"

"The same as always," says the shammes. "We wait for ten."

"Count me!" I say loudly.

"You don't count," says Schlomo.

The shammes laughs. "Sure, she counts. She's half-a-man."

Tsibble jumps up and down.

"Missus, Missus. I got trick."

He takes off his worker's cap.

"Winter. Head is cold. Now watch trick."

From his pocket he takes out a plastic sandwich bag, inserts it into the cap, and replaces the cap on his head.

"Now I warm. God bless America!"

Ralph, the reader, laughs.

Fred tells Rabbi Ornstein, "I missed *yarmulke* on the crossword puzzle yesterday. I spelled it with an *h*, and it should be an *r*."

Rabbi Ornstein tells Fred, "If you wore it more often, you'd know how to spell it."

Larry comes in. Everyone looks up. It's still not ten.

Larry holds his hands before him, fists closed.

"Which hand has the button?"

Fred teases him. "Larry, don't you know buttons are passé? It's Velcro, kiddo."

They get into a spirited argument, and I look at my watch. How will I get out of here on time?

Larry says, "Tell me, Fred, what have you got against the button, the metal button, the pearl button, the needle-wrought button, the engraved button, the cloth-covered button?"

"The rabbi's parking!" shouts Arnold, on a chair, looking out the window.

"Button up the space for him," says Larry.

"This place is full of nuts," says Fred. "Must be something in the air."

Fred grins at me.

"Macadamia, walnuts, peanuts. . . ."

Schlomo approaches Fred belly first. This is his stance since he has returned to Judaism.

"Fred, my man, let me have the mitzvah of teaching you to put on phylacteries."

Schlomo wraps the phylacteries, tefillin, seven times around Fred's left arm. Besides the leather thong, the tefillin have two little leather boxes containing strips of parchment with Hebrew Scripture, one strapped to the forehead and the other to the left arm. The men wear these every day but the Sabbath or holidays. I start when I first see the men, unicorned, and am aware that they are differentiated yet further from me.

Fred says, "I can never do that, Schlomo, without pinching my arm."

Schlomo says, "I'll show you. It's where your power lies."

Then Fred lets out a yelp.

"You pinched me!"

"Do it yourself!"

Fred says, "So I'm not such a good Jew."

Schlomo says, "There's no such thing as a bad Jew."

Fred says, "Schlomo, did you read in the paper that four landlords were arrested in Brooklyn, all Jews? One called Dracula."

"Must have been mitigating circumstances," says Schlomo.

Dad, I say, news item. Four Jewish landlords arrested in Brooklyn by District Attorney Elizabeth Holtzman. One is nicknamed Dracula for not making needed repairs. All have been fined many times and told to appear in court. They ignored summonses for lack of pest control, for exposed wiring, leaking plumbing, leaking roofs, and crippled elevators.

Mitigating circumstances, Dad?

Fred is about to tell the Dracula joke, where Dracula approaches his victim with his fangs bared; she holds up a cross, and he says in Yiddish, *Es vil dir gornischt helfen,* It won't help you any. We all groan.

"I've heard it a hundred times," says Schlomo.

"That's how you know it's a classic," says Fred.

The rabbi enters.

I read, amused, the blessing on being grateful for the orifices of the body, "marvelous in structure, intricate in design. Should but one of them, by being blocked or opened, fail to function, it would be impossible to exist." I am sure that after the recitation of this prayer, all the daveners are "regular."

We rise and sing, ". . . We are Your people, partners to Your covenant, descendants of Your beloved Abraham. . . . How blessed are we that twice each day, morning and evening, we are privileged to declare," and here we utter the Shema, "Hear, O Israel, the Lord our God, the Lord is One."

With no duties required from me in this room, with Hebrew coming so hard, I begin to make the prayers my own, rearranging the phrases, repeating lines:

> We are Thy people
> The children of the covenant
> We are Thy people
> The congregation of Abraham
> Happy are we

> How good is our destiny
> How beautiful our heritage
> Happy are we
> How goodly our portion
> How pleasant our lot
>
> Happy are we
> who rise up early
> to say how goodly
> how pleasant our portion
> how beautiful our heritage.

Fred sings tunelessly. The shammes ends it in his deep, gravelly voice:

> Happy are we
> who rise up early
> to say how goodly
> how pleasant our portion
> how beautiful our heritage
> happy are we
> who praise Thee.

The shammes shuffles over, chucking me under the chin.

"You'll learn to do that. You live long enough, you can learn anything. Every twenty years or so I learned a new profession, ending in the shammes business."

The rabbi is looking at his shammes and smiling.

Fred says, "The old geezer loves the ladies."

And my shammes laughs, "Love 'em and leave 'em, that's my motto."

You're not going to leave me so easily, Grandpa, I vow.

But Schlomo is watching this jealously.

"Rabbi, cover her since she's not modest enough to cover herself. I can't pray for my father with her face before me."

"Your face doesn't do much for me either, Bushy," I say.

The shammes stops us. "A motion. I want to introduce a motion. Everybody grow up!"

The rabbi tells Schlomo, "She's praying for her father also, Schlomo. Your father, he should be in peace, died long ago. It was then you should have prayed. I know you returned, but first you strayed."

"Rabbi, cover her," says bedecked Joshua.

The rabbi pulls the curtain on its wheels firmly in front of me.

"Don't, Rabbi! Don't pull that *schmata* across me!" I plead.

I cling to the clothes rack.

"It's the rule," says the rabbi. "Just a little, a little this way."

"It's not a little, Rabbi. You try standing behind it. You won't even feel like you're in the room."

"Young lady!" yells the shammes. "You think we got all day for your business? Kaddish!" he announces.

The rabbi holds out a piece of paper to me.

"I can give you a transliteration."

"I can learn the Hebrew." And I refuse his offering.

The rabbi sees the group slowing down, maybe tired from waiting for the minyan.

"Quick," he says, "like the Indianapolis Speedway, round the bend, and in no time we'll have schnapps and honey cake."

Leisure World, Saturday, January 17

If *aninut* is the first phase of mourning, we do not wail. We do not tear our hair. But I cried so, flying back across the country, that I never removed my sunglasses. My eyes still burn, my cheeks are chapped, my breath keeps catching.

In the parents' house, Mom and my brother Jay weep and lean into each other. They are too restrained to wail; they scarcely even whisper. Mostly they stand together in the silent house.

Leisure World, Week of January 16

The day before the funeral, my middle brother, Monte, joins us and we again discuss our remarks. Perhaps laughter is the other side of *aninut*. Monte chuckles as he tells the story that has become classic in our family:

The brothers, parents, and my family were in a posh restaurant in Detroit. It was my parents' fortieth anniversary. Monte gave the congratulatory toast.

"You have been married so long, so successfully," my middle brother said. "To what do you owe your success?"

Dad cleared his throat.

"Give in," he said, "but only on the important things."

These stories that we tell to one another will be repeated at the funeral. Most of the people in attendance will not have heard the family lore. They are the Leisure World contingent, acquainted with one another only in the last years of their lives.

I describe my father reading *Goldilocks and the Three Bears* to my nephew Mikey, who was then four years old. Dad reads the story and Mikey says, "Again, Papa." Patiently, with inflection, he reads *Goldilocks* again. In the tyrannical way of children, Mikey orders, "Again, Papa!"

My dad looks up at us, his small blue eyes twinkling, and says, "You know, I learn something new every time I read *Goldilocks.*" As if he were a scholar explicating text.

There is the story Dad told about Alte Sudvick:

A distinguished scholar, a cousin of my father's family, Sudvick the Elder, came from the Ukraine to Milwaukee. He could not find work as a Talmudic specialist. Finally, a landsman, who has become a peddler, sought to help.

"Some peddlers make a fortune, Sudvick," said the countryman. "I'll set you up with rags and a cart, and all you have to do is walk the streets and call, 'Rags for sale!'"

So Sudvick borrowed the money for the rags and the cart and gave the down payment to the cousin.

"Rise early," the cousin advised. "The early bird catches the worm."

Sudvick did not comprehend this ornithological information, but he rose at dawn.

He pushed the cart up and down the street and tried to remember what he was supposed to shout. He walked the streets like a *shtimme,* a dummy, from morning to late afternoon and never opened his mouth.

A policeman saw him coming down the sidewalk.

"What do you have there, old man?" asked the cop. "Rags?"

Sudvick was overjoyed.

"Rags! Rags!" he called and shook the policeman's hand.

I do not know what happened to Sudvick. I imagine he found a way to work, maybe at a sweatshop, and to study, perhaps at a corner shul, much like the one where I have been praying, surrounded by men like himself whose bodies and souls are separated in the New Land.

Leisure World, Week of January 16

THE MINYAN MEN

The time of *shivah* was a week of grace, largely because of the Minyan Men, the group of elderly gentlemen from the Leisure World Temple Judea, who came for kaddish at 8 A.M. and again at five for evening services.

They opened the folding chairs and set them up in rows. They would not accept our thanks because it was their mitzvah. They seldom ate or drank anything, maybe half a bagel, to make my mother feel better, and an eyecup of schnapps. They drank so they could give the necessary and only toast, *L'Chaim,* "To Life." They said the required phrase of comfort, "May you never know sorrow more."

The Minyan Men ranged in health, age, background.

Nate, a former entertainer, came every day in another outfit.

"Nate, I see you're a Texan today," said my mother.

Nate preened in his cowboy hat and string tie and leather belt.

"Nate, what's this outfit supposed to be?"

"Scottish," said Nate, in his tam-o'-shanter and clan tie.

Sometimes he was Frenchy with the navy blue tam and the turtleneck. For the remaining days of *shivah,* he would appear first as a Spaniard, then as a Brit.

"You're a whole United Nations, Nate," he'd be told, "a minyan by yourself."

There was Mike, handsome, energetic. Mike had a heart attack at sixty-four, went on the Pritikin diet, returned to Judaism, kept both diet and religion strictly, and remained healthy.

There was little Isidore, one of the first Jews to go to Harvard Law School, full of cute, corny ways.

"Look over there," he said to my daughter Sari.

She turned her head, and he quickly kissed her cheek.

"Shake hands," he said to my young nephew Mikey, and afterward Mikey found hard, wrapped candy in his own palm.

It was the articulate Mike who explained the absence of one or another of the group.

"Many are dreadfully ill or they have to take their wives to the doctor. Isidore isn't here today; he needs a blood test. Nate isn't here because he can't see well enough to walk since the cataract operation and no one picked him up this morning. But we have a good core group and you'll be covered."

It was Mike who talked to me about my father.

"A person goes along, and one day an angel whispers in his ear and old age suddenly sets in. That's how it was with your father, vigorous one day, a shuffling step the next."

The Minyan Men of Leisure World honored the ages, the beginnings and the endings. They played with the grandchildren, teased them, invited them to visit, got them scholarships to Hebrew camp or to study in Israel.

They called daily upon my mother. They, of the Ritual Committee, told us exactly what was expected of us as mourners. They put our lives into a context.

It was because of the Minyan Men in California that, upon my return to New York, I decided to say kaddish.

New York, Thursday, January 29

I am dining with, among others, a famous psychoan-
alyst. Our party meets for dinner at Sara Beth's on
Madison and Ninety-third. I am being taken to dinner
because I am a respondent for a meeting at a psycho-
analytic institute. I am responding to the great man's
paper on the *akida,* the biblical binding of Isaac. At the
table, the analyst shows us the cover of his book about
to be published, a work dealing with the subject of
love. His wife cuts his meat for him into bite-size
pieces, clearly an example of love.

The other respondents are his trainees, his
analysands.

They tremble, stutter, and perspire at the prospect
of commenting on their mentor's work.

As a novelist and academic, I cannot merely respond
to a paper. I build a structure of my own.

I rise to speak. The analyst, anticipating a paean to
his paper, cocks his head to listen. But I contradict,
dance around the analyst's concept. I have my own
story to tell, the chilling tale of trust and betrayal that I
hear each morning (Genesis 22:1–24).

I talk about the men with whom I spend my days,
from the ninety-five-year-old shammes of the shul to
the bewildered young men brought in off the street to
make a minyan. I tell how each of them knows that
when he raises his own eyes he will see the glint of the
knife and wonder about this terrible joke that his father, or Father God, is ready to play on him. The words
sacrifice and *blood* are often repeated.

I tell the gathered therapists, psychologists, psycho-
analysts that death is very close to us in the shul in the

mornings with the daily repetition of the story of the near-sacrifice, the *akida,* the binding of Isaac.

"Does each man, in turn, feel bound, tethered," I ask the audience, "in danger?"

I end, "There is something worse. That is to stand behind a curtain stretched on metal poles. Curtained or partitioned, I am invisible. Worse than the binding is this unbinding, this disconnection, this being pushed out of one's inheritance and chronicle."

When I step down, women crowd the podium to thank me. The analyst's wife regards me coldly. What do I know of love or of being bound?

I think of the synagogue. If death is the training of the minyan, going from father to son through the generation, then what am I doing in that tradition? If I voluntarily go to services, then, perhaps, like the Bedouin wives and concubines of our forefathers, indeed I should stand behind a curtain.

Some time later I think I see the famous analyst in a Woody Allen film.

New York, End of January

Each morning I sit on the woman's bench in plain view, pushing away the curtain. And each morning I am challenged, not only about the *mekhitza* but about everything else.

Will I move just a bit behind the curtain?

"Never," I say, attaching myself firmly to the bench, rolling the curtain on its wheels away from me.

Would I mind not getting my own prayer book, just waiting for it to be set on my bench?

"Never," I say, going to the cabinet.

Would I dress in seemly fashion, cease from wearing slacks this winter?

"Never," I say and go down to Macy's, which is having its winter sale on lined pants.

Whenever I say never, Tsibble turns his head, whistles, and applauds. At first I'm heartened, and then I wonder if he has any idea what's going on, for he has the same reaction when the shammes announces *kiddish* and schnapps. He's the first out the door. The shammes walks with his cane, calling, "Don't drink from the bottle, Tsibble. From the glass! From the glass!"

But once in a while he doesn't whistle and hoot and applaud. He starts sobbing.

"*Umgekumin, umgekumin, alle yidden umgekumin!*
Lost, lost, all the Jews lost!
Geshossen. Men hat zei geshossen!
Shot, shot. They were shot!*"

"Poor Tsibble," says the shammes. "Here are the Jews. We're not lost. We're not shot."

Tsibble isn't the only one. On Shabbos, in the main sanctuary, is a fellow with natty dress, a foolish grin, and nightmares that interrupt the Torah portion. Like Tsibble, he also speaks in Yiddish. Tsibble, however, can be in the present in English if he wishes. The fellow who comes only during the Sabbath thinks the Nazis won't understand or the enemies will not arrest him if he speaks in his secret code, in his *mamaloshen,* mother tongue.

This guy talks about having all his papers. He can show them to the police. He's a good citizen.

Now and then he disappears.

"Back to the loony bin," says Fred.

And he'll return on a Shabbos to scream out, "*Vas ich hab shoyn gesehen!* What I saw! In the church, shot dead. A woman of twenty, shot. A woman of forty, shot. A woman of eighty, shot. In the church."

"Pity him," says the rabbi, "still suffering from the Holocaust."

"It's getting boring already," says a cranky congregant. "So many of them."

Arnold, a lawyer who would rather be a sports announcer, is also unsympathetic.

"He knows when to act up," says Arnold. "He doesn't do it on an ordinary Shabbos but waits for a bar mitzvah, for strangers to be in the shul, and then he lets them have it."

"He gives me the heebie-jeebies," says Fred, who would rather laugh.

The shul is full of heebie-jeebies.

And in my daily group, there is the push and pull of the *mekhitza* on its clothes rack. Schlomo pulls it in front of me; I push it away.

The rabbi says, "Why does Schlomo get so excited? I told him, 'Leave it to me. I can make something work. A little golden thread will take care of it.'"

Is the rabbi about to tell a fairy tale with the magical properties of golden thread?

As the rabbi is leaning over me speaking, he cracks his ankle on the heavy wheels.

"A person could break something in this place," he says.

"Only the heart," I tell him.

We've been waiting half an hour or more all week for the tenth man.

One is dragged in today, a retarded young man, his head to one side, drooling. He's led to a front bench and sits there, his hands idle in his lap.

The shammes looks at him.

"At least give him a book," says the shammes. "He looks like a dummy sitting there."

"He *is* a dummy," says Fred.

The rabbi enters, looks around, and rubs his hands energetically.

"*Now* we have a minyan."

Daddy, are you laughing?

My dad would have shaken his head in amusement.

Esther, he would have said, don't let that material go to waste.

New York, End of January

Friends have written sweetly, have phoned with advice, have come to call with characteristic or uncharacteristic sharing.

Cecelia Musso, my chiropractor, has to treat not my back this morning, but my neck and head.

"What's rattling around in your head?" she asks.

"A coffin," I tell her.

"This will be an interesting time for you," she says. "Your father's voice will be close to you for almost three months. Be open to it. Listen intently."

She lost her parents two years ago, about the time I became her patient with chronic back pain.

"It takes about two years," says Cecelia, trying to release my tight neck muscles. "I still run after people thinking they're my mother, my father. I felt like an orphan, like someone from another planet, when they both died."

I am lying on her consulting table. My head appears to my touch to be bumpy and lumpy; my neck is stiff. It is all a metaphor. I am lopsided without both parents. I will return to her for another visit with yet another complaint.

Deborah Wolf, an anthropologist, says, "Your dad will keep coming to you in flashes, as mine did. You'll reconstitute him as you need him, and it will be that way the rest of your life."

I talk to an artist whom I met at MacDowell Colony when we were both "colonists" in Peterborough, New Hampshire.

"I thought the *shivah* would be for my father," the artist says. "But it was for me. It filled me with calm and sweetness. What you do, you aren't doing for your parents, but for yourself.

"There are compromises you make. You have a different sense of time, a more flexible one. You can spend hours contemplating. I suspect that your life may change forever as you learn to make space to mourn. So be gentle with yourself."

He is boyish in face and dress, wearing soft red shoes like an elf, and he looks as if the world of grief had never touched him.

I tell him, "My left breast pains me as though I bumped it. Then I thought maybe my heart was hurting."

"My two brothers and I had pains in the chest," says the artist, "but they left about two weeks after *shivah*."

My dear friend, the poet and novelist Paul Pines, writes:

At certain times, though I have now lived longer without him in my world than with him, I feel the loss of my father. I wish he were around to see [baby] Charlotte. My mother, also. I have learned to speak to them in myself—and sometimes they even answer.

Paul speaks of the knowledge "of such a loss—as well as the deepening that is part of the healing."

A great tenderness has come to me through my friends. The loss of a father has affected, especially, my men friends.

Bernard Weinstein, head of cancer research at Columbia Presbyterian, speaks of his love for his father. His father was a Yiddishist, active in the Socialist *Verein,* the Workman's Circle in Wisconsin.

"I had to sit through long speeches," says Bernie, "for my father was president of the Madison chapter. As a child in Workman's Circle camp, I would write letters to him in Yiddish. I only recently found them in my father's carefully kept archives. In my boyish handwriting, I would address them to *mein teyerer tateh.*

"I can hardly read them now," says Bernie. "The words have escaped. But, at night, even though I am a father of grown children, I call out, '*Tateh,* don't leave me,' though he died when I was twenty, decades ago."

We carry our fathers in our hearts or on our backs like Sinbad carried the old sailor. Bernie and his brothers have established a Yiddish music section at YIVO, the Yiddish institute in New York City.

And what will I carry on for my father? I think of dramatizing my parents' memoirs. I like the idea of the voices of my parents resounding, of an audience applauding their words and lives.

How mannerly and considerate friends are, beyond the obligatory note or condolence call. They send me art cards, bring books, nourishing soup, a rich chocolate cake.

Bikur Cholim, visiting the sick, is one of the mitzvahs, and I *am* sick, heart-sick.

Karl Schrag, the great artist, has been ill and is recovering. Nonetheless, Ilse and Karl send their wisdom, also a postcard, *Quai d'Orsay*, with a photograph by André Kertész, 1926. I am absorbed in it for an hour.

Because my time is simplified since I have limited my activities, I can stare at a postcard for an hour. As my artist friend anticipated, there is a flexibility to the day. I have compromised by deciding everything but shul and school is extraneous, except for the need to remember.

I have not listened to music, heard the radio, watched television, gone out casually, eaten at restaurants, met socially with friends, or attended films or plays, for in the month of *schlosshim* entertainment is forbidden the mourner. There are great spaces of silence. I am getting used to it. How will I let go of that kind of a day where I do a prescribed number of things, daven, teach, write, walk a little, make dinner, and receive the few callers?

I stare at the postcard from the Schrags. In this Kertesz photograph, workers, wearing their caps and working boots, approach the cameraman. A silver-haired gentleman with dark bowler, tailored dark coat, a silhouette of black, regards the workers. It is as if he were going across the *pont*, across this Parisian river, out of life.

Karl Schrag was recently looking off into that space. His latest paintings reflect a near-friendship with death. In a self-portrait, the fragile figure sits on the edge of the bed, the day already heavily upon him. But Karl, unlike my father, has returned to us.

Karl writes, "We are feeling that sadness with you. . . . One feels that spring comes closer. The sunlight on the sunny side of Lexington Avenue feels different."

I want to take attendance of all of my friends. Is everyone alive and well? I want no one to go on any journey without informing me of departure and return.

Everything is learning.

Saturday the 31st, over two weeks since my father died on Thursday, January 15, my friends from the women's community will come to share loss with me. I have been in another world and wish to explain it but not to make myself more important as a mourner than the one who has been taken.

∾

New York, End of January

Mom laughs over the phone. She is telling me about Dad's costumed friend Nate who has come visiting to pay his daily condolence call.

"He stays every afternoon for two hours," says Mom. "I told Nate I wanted to take a nap, but Nate said, 'I promised your children I'd look in on you. Paul and I were like brothers.'

"But Nate's not my brother. He leans on the bell for five minutes. I know his ring already. He's afraid I may be ill, may not hear him, may not want him, but he comes in, pushing past me when I finally answer, and sits for two hours not noticing if I nap or if dinner is burning on the stove."

I, listening from New York, am nevertheless grateful to Noogy Nate, one of the Minyan Men.

I hang up after loving good-byes. Like flashes, as Deborah Wolf said, my father comes to me, and I re-constitute him.

"*Tateh*," I want to cry, "don't leave me."

New York, Saturday, January 31

Lanni arranges a post-*shivah* where my friends who have lost a parent or have ailing parents come to inform me of how they mourned.

Several of us appear periodically to comfort, rejoice, celebrate, and designate a certain event important in a woman's life.

Both of Rose's parents died when she was a young woman.

"The time is never right," she says, as did the rabbi, "and what you do is never enough."

Michele speaks of her sorrow.

"My cheeks were chapped for a year from the salt of my tears. My ribs felt broken from crying. But you carry the good within them in you and you pass it on," says Michele, "and this I know fervently."

Michele tells about the fire that destroyed her mother's house and killed her mother.

"The firemen came and chopped and broke, and the backyard was full of my mother's little porcelain treasures. I washed the soot off them, cleaning the horns of the precious statue of a deer. These were her artifacts, important to her, so I treasure them, for I am the keeper of the documents."

I reach for her hand and she continues.

"The fire was shortly before Pesach. She had elegant Lalique French-carved glass dishes, and I set one small dish on the table to hold the saltwater, to hold my own tears."

Another friend also recently lost a parent, her mother.

"I didn't mourn enough," she says. "I can't get enough of grieving."

We, this post-*shivah* group, argue about New Age and middle age, past lives and new lives and atheism and my strange feminist rebellion of saying kaddish in an Orthodox shul. I can't quite explain it, but I try to tell them that the pain in my shoulder feels better when I am in the synagogue. I am not the only pallbearer.

Leah Napolin, who wrote the stage adaptation of the I. B. Singer story *Yentl*, speaks of absurdity, laughter, and tears in the burial of her father.

"We would visit him in the nursing home, and he would go to the door with us and want to follow us home," says Leah.

" 'Let me go with you,' he would cry.

"We would walk hastily, tears blinding our eyes, out the front door.

"'I'll get lost,' he would call after us, 'if I go alone.'

"The cemetery where he was buried was far from my father's home, and a distance from the nursing home. After the funeral, I thought I heard my father cry, 'I'll get lost if I go alone.'"

I no longer feel alone.

New York, Beginning of February

My sense of time is not linear. I had a repeated dream of what happened when I phoned my mother just after the death. My mother refused to speak to me.

"Is she angry," I asked my brother Jay, "that Dad got chilled the day we persuaded him to go to the pool?"

"No, no," Jay reassured me.

"Is she angry that I saw he was ill and didn't postpone my trip?"

"No," he said. "it isn't that."

"What is it?"

"She can't speak," Jay said. "It's simply that."

When I got to Leisure World, my mother's arms were wide open and pulled me to her, against her.

Why do I continue to dream this? Because I don't accept the death? Because I fear that death is rejection? Because I feel guilty that my father became chilled after he reluctantly took me swimming? Because I think mother blames me also?

Yet that final embrace is forgiveness. And how long will she be there to forgive me?

New York, Monday, February 2

A meeting of the Deborah Project.

I ring the bell at 7:30 on West Seventy-sixth Street. We meet at the West Side apartment of the organizer and playwright Susan Nanus.

The Deborah Project was started with great hoopla by the theater department of the Ninety-second Street YM/YWCA. The purpose is to listen to the voices of Jewish women playwrights and to perform their plays.

Besides Susan's apartment, we meet at the theater downstairs when there is no performance or rehearsal, and we read and critique one another. Directors, actors, and writers are there. Our plays will be performed in staged reading at a spring festival.

The Deborah Project cannot possibly know, despite the three years we've been together, that the Y is no longer taking theater seriously, and Jewish women even less so.

One director after another is fired. The board of the Y, largely businessmen, sees no need for its long-running commercial theater or for the new, innovative Mosaic Theater under the direction of Michael Posnick or for our own Deborah Project, women's theater.

There is always Broadway, off-Broadway, off-off Broadway. Seek your fortune elsewhere, we're as good as told. As the stage lights dim on us, we notice that fewer and fewer women are onstage in any of the programs of the Ninety-second Street Y.

𝕽

New York, Tuesday, February 3

I have invited Vivian Gornick to read at the Westchester college.

She is reading from *Fierce Attachments,* her memoir about the mother-daughter relationship. It is a lucid and passionate book. I know it intimately, for she read it to me in progress every Sunday night last year.

𝕽

New York, Wednesday, February 4

Dad, I said, Liberace died.

My dad would have replied sarcastically, I'm sitting *shivah* for him.

Bob is buying a set of drafting drawers to store his large output of prints. The drawers cost $475 and will house monoprints, silkscreens, lithographs, and etchings. There are also collage fabric and photo-engraved pieces.

Bob arranges his work in the drawers by size and technique. Each drawer that he pulls open is like a window shade snapped up on the colors of a bright day.

New York, Tuesday, February 10

Sitting on my bench, which *is* the women's section, I read ancient prayers. I obey or disobey the customs. Sometimes there is more anger than comfort. But I am spending this time of *schlosshim*, the thirty days, in thinking.

The rabbi has mentioned a golden thread and that he will solve Schlomo's problem with me and with the *mekhitza*. He is as good as his word.

The new *mekhitza* is in place. From the ceiling on golden threads hangs a curtain rod and, from that, cheap lace doubled over. It is positioned carefully over my bench. I cannot push it aside. The men cannot be aware of me unless I poke my head forward or stand in front of the curtain. Otherwise, I am shadowy to them and they to me.

It is time to take out the Torah. Rabbi Ornstein is carrying the Torah around this tiny room. I reach out to touch it, but he holds it away from me, my hand still stretching out as the Torah in its velvet casing goes marching past me.

I am enraged. They think they can get away with everything, and often they can. Even keeping the sacred writings away from me. Not that I am a true believer, but to clutch one's history, one's text, and keep it out of the grasp of women is what this seems to be about.

Fred speaks to me after services.

"Don't be upset," he says. "There'll be a whole parade of Torahs in your life. Go to the nice shul on Gramercy Park. They love the ladies. The ladies run everything there from soup to nuts. Nuts!" Fred never stops joking even when he's saying something tender. "Filberts, almonds."

I'm slow packing up to go.

"Listen," Fred asks me, "you want to go outside, have coffee, a bran muffin, a *cruller*, sugar doughnut?"

I smile at him but shake my head. I'm off to my studio to write.

"How about croissant?" asks Fred. "Cornflakes? Hot oatmeal? Grits?"

"No! No!" I laugh.

"*Matzo brei?*" asks Fred. "Poached eggs on whole wheat?"

"I'm busy today, Fred," I say.

"You're always busy," he says and is about to turn away when he tries again.

"What about the library? I'll treat you to a book."

"I have a book, Fred."

"Then how about some fast walking and fast talking?" asks Fred.

There is a certain sexual tension in this small room, even early in the morning. The men eye me, make suggestive remarks, pet me when they're not on the attack. I, as the only woman, receive too much attention, either wrathful or wistful. Fred's is wistful.

"Well," says Fred, "don't worry. This could be my day for the annual checkup. Or maybe the dental hygienist left a message on my answering machine for a cleaning."

"Maybe, Fred," I say. "And maybe another time."

The men jam the corridor and begin arguing about the decreasing membership.

"Give women equal rights," I say. "You'll have more members."

They ignore me.

"Comes a holiday, it's a barren landscape out there," says Rabbi Ornstein. "We have to be *frumer*, more religious."

"Listen, I got a story will cheer you up," says Fred, "fresh from the farmer's market."

57

He blocks the door.

"This is a Miami Beach joke," he says, trying to hook me. "I used to go to Miami Beach every winter."

"You're not going this winter, Fred?" I ask.

"Nobody to pack for me," says Fred lightly and launches into the joke.

> There's an older woman sitting at the poolside. She looks up and sees an older man, who is also sitting on the edge of the pool. But he's pale, very pale, like a slug.
>
> She says, "Pardon me, Mister. How come you look like that?"
>
> He replies, "I've been in prison."
>
> "You've been in prison? For what, may I ask?"
>
> "For murdering my wife. Brutally."
>
> She says to him, "Does that mean you're single?"

The men laugh, and I wonder if Fred is telling me that a single man can get away with anything.

New York, Wednesday, February 11

In three more days I end *schlosshim*. What has happened to me, to my mourning and sense of commitment?

Sitting behind the *mekhitza* or standing beside it, I keep my eyes down-turned. I hear whispers and am certain they are speaking about me. I never know who will speak so. Is the friendly fellow who greets me with "Hi ya, Es" also telling the rabbi, "Maybe she'll go to another shul"?

I have disturbed some of the regulars, especially those cursed by Doris: Schlomo, the returned Jew;

Ornstein, a rabbi without congregation; Joshua, trying too hard to be one of the Orthies.

There are others, not necessarily part of this cabal, like Gray Braid, always in sixties garb, or the Professor, a stern martinet, who covers his face with his long, fringed tallis and turns his back upon me when he prays. If he has poked his head out of the tallis, if the Professor happens to pass and catches my eye, he flicks his tallis at me. I feel as if I were being shooed away like some farm animal.

When the cabal is in the majority I have a terrible time getting an Amen as I recite kaddish. There are variations on the Mourners' Prayer that require Amens after each paragraph or the mourner cannot go on.

My recitation is followed by silence. Fred turns around, sees no one about to join me, and says loudly, "Amen." The shammes and the rabbi belatedly join in.

I dread the day when I pray and there is silence. But then, is it superstition? My father can handle his own, morally or ethically.

My father's thick glasses would enlarge his sunken eyes, and he would say, "God will hear your voice and He will say Amen."

Nobody Up There was listening on the day of the attack.

This past week Ornstein approached me and said, "You are misbehaving in my house. We are Orthodox here and do not allow women to show their faces."

I look unblinkingly at him. I stand away from the curtains on their golden thread.

"There's no separation of women in the main sanctuary," I say. "You're being inconsistent and hypocritical."

"Listen, lady," he says, "you have no business here."

"I have as much business as you," I say. "And this is not your house."

He is enraged. "Lady, there's no place for you here," he says.

"You have nothing to say about it," I say and try to open the prayer book, but he pulls loose the curtain from the rack, throws it over my head, and seems to be attempting to strangle me.

It's so startling—this small room to be the scene of such melodrama!

"Get out, lady," he's yelling.

I give him the knee and pull loose.

"Don't call me lady," I yell back, as nuts as he is. "Call me doctor."

"I know what I'll call you, *zonah,* whore," he says.

The men in the room are startled. That is not a word thrown around lightly. The jokester Fred looks unusually serious. Larry, the retired button man, nods at me to have courage when, flushed, I try to continue with the service.

The Professor shakes his head at both of us.

"Two wrongs do not make a right," he says, turning his back on both houses.

At the same time, Ornstein stamps out noisily. Joshua follows, showily kissing the mezuzah on the doorpost as he makes his exit. Gray Braid closes the prayer book that he's been vaguely staring at and follows.

I am becoming an uncivilized person in these surroundings, profane, disrespectful, prejudiced. All that I am is being altered.

A cabal forms that lasts the winter and spring.

New York, Thursday, February 12

Today Bob has flown to Boston for a College Art Association national meeting. He has marked in his catalogue two panels to attend, one on postmodern narrative painting and another on printmaking.

Bob flies out at 8 A.M. and returns to LaGuardia after midnight. He is leaving me alone in the clutches of the shul.

In the meantime, the rabbi of the synagogue is concerned. More than anything he wants *shalom bayit*, peace in the house. But without his regulars, how will he ever get up a minyan? He has lost Ornstein, Joshua, Schlomo, Gray Braid, the Professor, and others who have started an earlier minyan in order not to have me in their midst. The new minyan meets an hour earlier, 6:45 A.M. The men occasionally peek into ours on their way out the door, pleased by our sparse attendance.

The rabbi phones the grocer or the hotel manager, or he stands by the front door, leaving it slightly ajar, and tries to hook a fish. His life is not easy.

The Professor, if prevailed upon by the rabbi to be the tenth man in our minyan, davens in the corridor, pacing back and forth like some disturbed ghost under his great prayer shawl. One or another of the earlier group peers into the davening room and, upon catching a glimpse of me, refuses to enter.

Schlomo is in full dress regalia, white unbuttoned shirt, dark suit, close-fitting black hat, yeshiva garb, though he's never been to yeshiva. He is whispering to my rabbi. About me? Yes. He speaks out.

"If you want us back, Rabbi, you'll have to choose."

"Choose what?" asks the rabbi.

"Choose between a man and half-a-man."

Seeing Schlomo engaged in conversation with the rabbi, Joshua is emboldened to enter the prayer room. He leans across the curtain, his shirt sleeves rolled up and the phylactery wrapped around his left arm.

"Don't you know the difference between men and women?" he asks me. "You're an educated woman. I shouldn't have to explain to you that this is the way it is, this is the law of the separation of man and woman. You've got to obey the law."

I whisper back, "Joshua, don't send me to the back of the bus."

"Bitch!" he says.

I begin to feel my skin prickle. I am the only member of a minority present. No matter who or what a man is, in these quarters he is, at the least, acceptable and, at best, superior.

Does Joshua, who rejects my presence here, elsewhere think of his skin as ill-fitting? Does he hear whispers and try to sit more and more compactly, as has become my wont?

This night I ask Bob, as I look in the mirror and tentatively touch my face, if he sees fur growing on me.

New York, Friday, February 13

I daven in the morning and am a witch in the evening.

In the morning the rabbi is boasting.

"You come to shul," he tells the guys, "you don't get a stomachache. Shul cures everything. You know that old guy used to bend way over, his tallis swept the ground? Herb what's-his-name. Osteoporosis he had, bent double, but attended regularly and his posture improved. He was as erect as me when he left us."

"Where did he go?" I ask.

"He died," says the rabbi.

"But with good posture," adds Fred.

The rabbi says, "Don't laugh. Who cured polio? A Jew. Before you know it, a Jew will find the cure to

AIDS. Look at our Morning Benedictions, our washing up, our prayers for cleanliness. Even so far back we were of a scientific turn of mind."

The shammes wants us to get back to business.

"In the meantime," he says, "back to the ranch. 'How goodly are thy tents, O Jacob.'"

He shuffles to me and taps my prayer book.

The shammes is gleeful. He loves the song we're about to sing, "The Song of Moses." He sings out in his husky, gravelly voice, *Az yashir Moshe,* "Thus sang Moses." I taste it like a poem and paraphrase it.

> The chariots of Pharaoh
> He cast into the sea
> The captains of Pharaoh
> Into the Red Sea
> And the depths covered them.
>
> They went down like a stone
> They sank like lead in the waters
> The horse and rider
> are thrown into the sea
> They went down like a stone
>
> Deep in the sea
> Still as a stone
>
> With His strong right hand
> with His hand he shattered them
> He stretched out his hand
> the earth swallowed them
> the army is still as a stone
>
> Thus sang Moses
> and the children of Israel.

The shammes smiles. "Now that's a song with some meat on it. The bad guys lose, the good guys win, and we're the good guys!"

P.M.

Harriette Hartigan is driving in from Connecticut.
She is a photographer, midwife, and journeyperson
through life.

We were friends in Detroit since the early years of
the women's movement. Harriette had agoraphobia
when I first met her. I could persuade her to leave the
house only once a week, in her beat-up blue van, to
drive me into the suburbs, where I lectured on literature for a woman's book club.

She'd pull up in the van near my apartment building
on campus.

"Climb into the Blue Mama," she'd say.

I needed Harriette both for the chauffeuring and
the support in hostile territory.

Although many of the women book clubbers read
ardently, were always prepared with the assignment
and ready to raise their hands, they would much have
preferred reciting to a male professor.

In the seventies a good share of the women were adjunct to other people, wives to professional husbands,
chauffeurs to busy children. If the women gave themselves office or studio space, it was in the basement of
their spacious homes, near the furnace room.

How could they, so hidden in their own lives, be
sympathetic to the new women's literature?

And Harriette and I epitomized all that frightened
them. I would wear my leather, broad-brimmed cowboy hat. Harriette would sport her cowboy boots, her
long straight hair falling in her face. We were the city,
bringing danger into the room.

We would park in front of the suburban home, sitting in the Blue Mama, while Harriette uncorked a
cheap bottle of wine, which we chug-a-lugged until we
felt it was the right time to encounter the group. I tried

to loosen them up occasionally, even bringing records with me, Cris Williamson or some other wonderful singer.

"Dance!" I ordered.

Only Harriette and I danced.

However, at the end of the course, when I reviewed Marilyn French's *The Women's Room*, the elegant house near the golf course where the book club was meeting was jammed. These women knew that no matter who they were—doctors', lawyers', or realtors' wives—they, like the characters of the novel, were still at risk.

Since then, Harriette has ventured forth bravely, documenting birth and death. She is my guide across both rivers, the briny river of Life, and Lethe, the still waters of the Underworld.

The day before my *schlosshim* ends, Harriette is here to console me. She has been saying farewell to a friend in Florida who is suffering from cervical cancer. Harriette drove down to hear her dying words.

"Death is a great teacher," says Harriette.

We go off in another old car. The Blue Mama has died.

Leisure World, Week of January 16

"Remember, Mama, when Dad said I couldn't be a newspaper reporter?"

"He said they talked dirty at the *Times*," my mother says.

Dad worked for the *Detroit Times*, a Hearst paper.

"I've gone from bad to Hearst," he used to joke.

"Remember Vera of the woman's page?" I ask.

Mother always laughed easily. Even now she manages to laugh. Talking about Dad makes her want to smile or cry.

"He liked her but she shocked him," says my mother. "He would tell me that in hot weather she would take off her dress and sit in her slip. But she always wore a hat because a professional woman wears a hat."

We laugh.

"Remember what he would say about Vera?" Mom asks.

"Yes. Dad said, 'Vera would not call a spade a spade. She called it a God-damned shovel.'"

Mom says, "He loved being a newspaperman."

"It wasn't all fun and games, though," I say.

"No," says my mother. "Like the time the House Un-American Activities Committee came to town."

Dad did not talk about that time, but his wrath over that period during the fifties took up the longest chapter in his memoir.

"Your father was a brave man," says my mother. "It was during the Red scare. The HUAC asked him to tell on a very nice young fellow who worked the copy desk with him. Paul loved that young man, and he and his wife and new baby were always at our place. Then those people came to town to make trouble. First thing, they call up your father to question him about this young man.

"'I won't rat on anybody for you,' said your father. And he told them, 'Go to hell!'"

I clap.

"Don't applaud. It wasn't so easy. The young man was fired and your father was called in by the managing editor and told, 'I can get rid of you just the same way.'"

"But he never ratted."

"Never," says my mother. "And a wonderful thing happened. He tried to keep in touch with that young newspaperman but lost track of him. One day he saw this man's name quoted in a newspaper, and the article said what newspaper the fellow worked for. Your father wrote to the paper. Sure enough, it was the same fellow, by now editor of a fine newspaper in Madison, Wisconsin. He'd had some hard years, he wrote your father, but finally there was a break, a chance to be a reporter on a liberal paper. From there he made it to editor and finally managing editor. He thanked your father for his friendship and his courage."

We sit quietly. Sometimes during this week I sleep with her, my head on the pillow where my father slept. She sleeps quieter that way.

"I was thinking of Moline, Illinois," says my mother in the darkness of the bedroom. "How brave your father was then also. He worked for a tri-state newspaper—Rock Island, Moline, and Davenport, I think they were. I don't have his memory. But, it was a long time ago. So the tri-state papers assigned him to work on the High Holy Days. Of course, he refused. They decided to make a big thing of it, can you imagine? They insisted. And they had might on their side. It was the Depression. Your dad realized he could lose this job and not get another. Still, he refused.

" 'It's a matter of principle,' your father told the editor. And he was fired."

"Did he get another job?"

"He did. And he was fired from that one too."

"How come?"

"It was 1927 in Evansville, Indiana. Could it have been the *Evansville Courier*? One newspaper sounds like another to me. It was a historic time. Sacco and Vanzetti, the anarchists, had just been killed. That very day, your father was on makeup. Without permission from the higher-ups, he put a black border around the front page."

"I'm proud of him," I say.

"Well, he was out of work for a long time after that," says Mama, "and we had to leave Evansville and go live with my family in Detroit. Courage costs."

New York, Saturday, February 14

Valentine's Day. It is the end of *schlosshim.* I am about to enter the fourth phase.

During *aninut,* we wept uncontrollably, only answering the door for other family members.

We sat *shivah,* obeying its prohibitions, the pillows removed from the couch and the mirrors covered, for one must not find comfort in pillows or seek vanity by looking into the mirror. Our feet were unshod so we would not be tempted to pursue business and go out of the house of mourning.

Schlosshim was quiet except for the students at the seminar or in appointments in my office. I wore my black ribbon pinned above my heart all this month, and the world around me hushed itself.

I am now into the remaining ten months of mourning, but I shall miss the time in my life when quiet reigned and I could think only of my father.

New York, Monday, February 16

The rabbi addresses the minyan as they remove the leather thongs of the tefillin from their left arms. He does not look in my direction. He says that Torah is read on Mondays and Thursdays because those were the traditional market days in *Eretz Israel*, the land of our ancestors. On those days the rabbis could reach the largest audience.

The rabbi continues, "People think that only the Arabs have market days on Mondays and Thursdays. That was *our* custom."

So who cares? I think idly as I remove the bobby pin holding my yarmulke in place. Whose custom is falafel and hummus?

The rabbi is suddenly off on a tangent.

"It is in the nature of Islam to want vengeance, in the heart and soul of the Muslim. In his blood!" he cries.

I stop. I am dressed for departure, carrying my briefcase.

"We should daven for peace and not for the sharpening of swords," I say. "As it is written in Isaiah, 'And nations shall know war no more.' "

The rabbi, really a most pleasant man, shifts his gaze from me. I have come out in front of the *mekhitza*. I am too noisy, opinionated. I have grown uncontrollably tall like Alice after she's drunk the magic potion. I seem to tower over the partition. He longs for my departure.

"Have a good weekend," says the shammes, who has remained silent.

"But it's not the weekend," I protest. "It's only Monday."

Tsibble hops around my bench and sings, *"Montag, Dienstag, Mitvoch,"* Monday, Tuesday, Wednesday.

"Come back tomorrow," he says. "Come back day after tomorrow. Come back."

Ralph, the serious young man, is laughing.

Is the shammes disappointed that I'll be returning too soon, or am I becoming paranoid? Perhaps he's becoming forgetful. But who has a better right?

Fred hangs around and hurriedly tells a joke. It is his uncomfortable and shy way of making contact with me, saying nothing personal, just telling stories, touching my elbow and walking off.

"Do you know this one?" asks Fred.

God created the earth, and in the course of time the earth went its own way with Adam and Eve and animals and history and wars and destruction. Then, the final destruction, nuclear holocaust!

God above looks down in horror at the devastation below.

"Take your eyes off them for one second . . . ," He says.

Does Fred think disaster will strike in this place unless he keeps his eye on me?

New York, Wednesday, February 18

Bob and I take out a family membership at the YMCA. We need to exercise and cool off. After shul I phone Bob and we meet at the Y. I need some of that River Jordan.

We swim for half an hour. Bob is having trouble catching his breath. Water is not the place of his comfort. He clutches the side of the pool, panting. I swim back and forth easily, go to dress, then suddenly turn, twist, and totally wreck my back.

"What's on your back?" asks my chiropractor, Cecelia Musso.

Only a couple of thousand years, Cecelia.

Later that day I hear that my friend Rose has had an accident, and I visit her at home. Rose has slipped on the ice and damaged the cartilage of her midriff. Her breasts are turning blue.

"We're some pair," says Rose, clutching her chest.

I, having hobbled in, sit carefully on the edge of a hard, straight-backed chair.

"Your neck is stiff?" Rose asks. "You got a pain in the neck? Your back is out? You're carrying the world on your shoulders, my good friend."

P.M.

Back troubles or not, *schlosshim* has ended and friends are having a performance, *In the Traffic of the City,* directed by and starring Arthur Strimling and written by the poet Mark Kaminsky—both of the Ballad Theater.

Traffic is a dramatic narrative composed of the tales of the Nagasaki survivors, a story of everyday life interrupted by devastation. I am ending the silence of *schlosshim* with strong stuff.

The director and author are concerned with the politics of survival and also with storytelling. They are disciples of the late anthropologist Barbara Myerhoff, who had gathered tales from the Yaqui Indians, the Jewish elderly in Venice, California, and the Hasidic community of Fairfax, Los Angeles.

It is Myerhoff's concept that the story echoes, deepens in the telling and retelling, changing both the teller and the hearer.

I wanted my students to learn about storytelling. I assigned Myerhoff's *Number Our Days.*

"Why are we reading this?" asked the students.

They didn't say it, but I knew they were wondering what they had in common with the poor elderly Jews of Venice, California.

How do you tell young people, who are unsure of who *they* are, that if they want to be witnesses, writers in their own time, they must be everybody?

New York, Thursday, February 19

A new *mekhitza* is in place.

First the clothes rack, then the curtain hanging from golden thread, now this new separation, the third *mekhitza*.

"It will please everyone," says the rabbi.

I enter out of breath from hastening to the synagogue.

I stop when I see the separation, not curtains but shower curtains, hanging from shower hooks.

The davening room is quiet as the men await my reaction. This is midweek and I am not teaching. Instead, I am going to the Y, carrying my string bag with bathing equipment. I open the bag and reach inside among the towel, suit, and shampoo for my bathing cap. I tuck my hair into the white cap, open the shower curtains, and daven.

Tsibble giggles. The others are stunned.

I resolve to carry sharp little scissors with me to poke holes into the shower curtains.

I also resolve to change my style of dress. There are sales at Macy's on outerwear. I will, as Schlomo warns, "dazzle" them from behind this opaque curtain.

New York, Friday, February 20

I have gone midtown to Macy's and bought outerwear in Day-Glo colors. I have jackets and a coat: one jacket a phosphorescent purple, the other jade green leather. My raincoat is a glorious, garish orange. I am in orange today, and the men blink when they gaze in my direction. They cannot dull me.

No wonder Orthodox women often dress smartly. It's one way to fight invisibility.

Tsibble, the garment worker, comes to me.

"Nice, lady, very nice."

I feel less and less nice.

At *kiddish* the men chase the crumbs of bagels around the table.

"You don't have to worry about hunting season in that coat," says our sports fan.

"You could stand in the dark and light up the room," says the joker.

"You could stop traffic," says the button man.

Fred has a joke for us over munchies. It's one of his Miami jokes. He used to vacation there with his "lovely lady," his much-missed wife, but goes nowhere on holiday these last two years since her death.

> A grandmother is babysitting in Miami Beach. She dresses her only grandson in a little swimsuit and sun hat. She watches him digging in the sun. The sky darkens, a summer storm comes up suddenly. A great wave pounds onto the shore and envelops the little boy.
>
> The *bobbeh* raises her arms to heaven and cries, "God, who are you doing this to? Don't I keep kosher? Don't I go to shul? To me you're doing this?"
>
> The rain stops, the sea calms, a great wave returns the little boy.
>
> The grandmother looks him over carefully, rises, looks upward, and says, "There was also a hat."

Is Fred saying I'm not satisfied to have been washed up on shore?

In the meantime, the history of the shower curtains, punctured by tiny scissor holes, is short-lived.

₪

New York, Sunday, February 22

The men often use the women's bench as a cloakroom, so that I find myself surrounded by coats, hats, scarves, gloves, rubbers. They don't want to befoul their own nest, all the other benches of the prayer room.

A full bench for me is too much. I take to bunching their outerwear at the corner of the bench and to laying one of my own brilliant jackets over theirs. They complain but continue to pile their discarded coats right up against me.

They also use this bench designated for women as the resting place for the silver *pushke*, the charity box. It seems to be such a useful bench for holding everything but women. When I enter I perform the daily, ongoing ritual of shoving a coat out of my way, removing the large cushion on which the *pushke* rests, and placing them on the men's side. I am angry even before the prayers begin.

Today, after watching this ritual, this bench cleaning, Fred comes to my side, leans over me, and compliments me on my bright jacket.

"I wish I had the courage to wear loud clothes," he said. "But I'm shy. I respect your bright outfit."

I know he's saying he cannot talk out loud before the others but recognizes my right to take a stand.

Leisure World, Before January 15

Before Dad dies I consult him about my writing projects.

"What's happening with the labor book?" he asks.

"I can't seem to solve it," I confess.

"You'll solve it," says my mother. "You always solve it."

"It isn't working," I address my father.

Too much motherly faith in me isn't helping at this moment when I am confronting failure in a project that I researched for years.

"What's wrong?" he asks.

"I can't create believable characters," I tell him.

"A pity," says my dad. "The material is so rich. And it's my time."

He looks at me wistfully.

"You know, I could help you do your research. I could get a bus to Los Angeles and use the downtown library."

"You can't find your way to Club House Four here in Leisure World," says my mother, "and suddenly you're Christopher Columbus going to find Los Angeles?"

I am moved by my father's offer. It was he who published the first labor newspaper in Michigan, who wrote speeches for labor-supported candidates, who helped to outfit them in respectable clothes for their campaigning. He even succeeded in electing pro-labor congressmen like old John Dingell, the father of the present Michigan congressman.

Now Dad wants to be a researcher for me.

"I'm thinking of giving it up," I say.

"Don't!" begs my father. "Use the material another way. Think of the heroines we knew in the labor movement, like Genora Dolinger and how she helped to launch the UAW. She was our own Joan of Arc."

"You'll work it out," says my mother. "You always do."

I don't always work it out, and now my dad is no longer available as a researcher.

᠗

New York, Sunday, February 22

Fred tells another joke.

Irving wants to win the Lotto lottery. He looks in the paper one day, another day, one week, another week, month after month.

He prays, "Please, God, let me win today."

He does not win.

"Why, O Lord?" he cries. "Why not me? Why can't I win the Lotto like all the others?"

The sky parts, there is a great light, and a voice thunders, "Irving, meet me halfway. Buy a ticket!"

᠗

New York, Monday, February 23

Dad, I say, news item. Date: February 23. Dateline: Washington.

Reagan tells the Tower panel that he can't remember approving the arms sale to Iran.

My dad would have said, Why should he concern himself with details?

Today I am sighing because of the synagogue. After this morning I have decided to daven at home, to leave the house of worship—a male house.

The fourth *mekhitza* is there, doubled-over lace curtain, hanging from the previous shower hooks.

Schlomo, hippie turned Hasid, tells the rabbi he wants to say kaddish for his father but he can see my face and it spoils it for him.

"Schlomo," says the rabbi, "you should have said kaddish years ago when your father died. But, all right. You're trying."

Suddenly the rabbi's face is before me, his hand upraised. I duck, thinking he is going to strike. He does, in a way. He draws the drapes. On the other side, the men are shadows. I, on my side, must also be a shadow.

A shower hook slips so that the rabbi is stuck there attaching it while I try to say my own kaddish, distracted by his hovering over me.

I leave the shul chilled, as if a funereal sheet were being pulled over my face or a bridal veil tied over my head or chador hung over my entire body.

New York, Wednesday, February 25

A.M.

News item, I tell my dad. Source: the *New York Times*. Dateline: Nairobi, Kenya. Writer: James Brook.

Dad always taught me the five *w*'s: who, what, when, where, why.

Mom called it his "Woo woo."

Who, I inform Dad, are the Kikuyu versus the Luos.

What, are warring tribal and modern values.

In Kenya a wealthy lawyer named S. M. Otieno died. He came from a tribal background, the Luo, but has had nothing to with his tribe.

For many years he lived not on tribal land but in a fashionable suburb of Nairobi. Otieno's widow, Virginia Wamabui Otieno, a political activist with the Mau Maus since she was seventeen, is of a different tribe, the Kikuyus. She does not want to give his body to the Luos but rather wants to bury her husband on his farm in the Ngong Hills near Nairobi.

The Luos say that Otieno's restless ghost will torment his survivors. They fear that he will be buried in a suit instead of in tribal garb. They are quoted:

"He will haunt his children, demanding to know why they allowed him to be buried there . . . in a tie. He screams that the tie is choking him."

The Luos say of the widow, "She is not relevant. She is a wife, a woman."

The court finds for the Luos. In the photograph accompanying the article, the Luos are dancing in the streets of downtown Nairobi. They will soon triumphantly take the body away from his family.

Dad, it could happen here. They're all Luos in this room.

A friend, a former member of the Israeli Knesset now living in Berkeley, sends me an article from an Israeli newspaper. There is a photo of a rabbi clad in white, with long white beard, pointing his finger threateningly at the daughter and wife of a man they are burying.

"Women have no place in the cemetery!" he thunders.

Ghostly in pale face and attire, he chases the deceased's family out of the cemetery, away from sanctified grounds, lest they defile the place.

More Luos, Dad, I say, and here I am defiling this place.

Mary Gordon spoke at the Forty-second Street Public Library on spirituality in art. She left two tickets for my colleague Linsey Abrams and me.

Mary lectured on the dualism and abstractionism in the church and said that the Catholics are underrepresented in the arts in this country because the Irish are obsessed with secrecy.

"If they tell you something, they say right afterward, 'Mind you, I've said nothing, hear?'" says Mary.

Mary Gordon's first book, *Final Payments*, told the secrets and we heard them.

I think of my first writing teacher from decades ago, Virginia Sorenson, who told the secrets of the Mormon Church.

I will lecture my students tomorrow that writing is about telling secrets and that each group has its secrets to tell. The secrets of women are being told. The secrets of African Americans are being told. The secrets of the Asian and Hispanic communities are beginning to be told. There are some secrets that are already public, too often told. But other secrets are whispered in the air, just waiting for an audience.

Do I have secrets from behind the curtain?

New York, Thursday, February 26

Davening at home requires more discipline than I seem to possess. First I exercise, then I clear the dishes and counter. By that time, I have to get to my job or the Writers' Room, and father is left unattended. I return to the synagogue.

All the men gather around the sacred scroll. It is left uncovered for a moment, and the men gently place the velvet covering over it.

"It's like a woman," the rabbi tells me. "It cannot be naked. It has to be clothed to be respected."

I am startled by that as well as the scene that follows.

The men rock the Torah in their arms. They caress it as they carry it around our little room. They pet it as if it were being burped, holding it rolled and scrolled over their shoulders.

They love the Torah—its words, the calligraphy of the revelations, even the *yad*, the silver pointer, that keeps the place. What is more, they are all actors in the drama around the Torah. It is an honor to have an *aliyah*, a chance to come up to perform some ritual act involving the Torah. They shake hands with one another for their accomplishments in reading, holding the heavy Torah aloft, even in rolling it up, belting it, and dressing it. After each action, the congregation shakes the hand of the man who performed the duty and calls out, *Y'yasher ko-akh*.

"What is *Y'yasher ko-akh?*" I ask the shammes.

He lifts his fist to the heavens.

"More power to you. May the Lord strengthen you."

But I am unemployed in these most sacred, most ancient of tasks.

The rabbi asks each of the men surrounding him the names of those for whom they're saying kaddish. I keep trying to say my father's Hebrew name and his father's name: Paltiel ben Yaakov.

They have already rejected his mother's name,

Tsivia (gazelle). There is only patrilineage. Jewish mothers may get big press, but not in the shul.

Today I wonder if they'll remember to call out to me for my father's name. After asking all the men, the rabbi at last remembers me, turns, and mispronounces the name for which I am in mourning and that I have repeated to him every day for three weeks now.

What am I doing here pretending I'm my Dad's kaddish and heir?

Would my father have said, "But, Esther, my two sons are my kaddish"?

This day in February I am angry not only that my father is dead, but also that, though I am the eldest, there is no primogeniture for daughters.

Bob says, "Don't give up. Don't let them make you give up. Think of Martin Luther King and Medgar Evers."

"They didn't give up," I say, "and look what happened to them."

On my days off I have a treat, the YMCA, after the heated waters of the minyan room. There Bob joins me at the pool, set on the thermostat for cool.

New York, Last Week of February

One morning this week, I forget the exact date, the trio, Schlomo, Joshua, and Ornstein, has been prevailed upon by the rabbi to attend both the earlier and the later minyanim.

Joshua enters first. Only he and I are in the minyan room.

He leans forward, as I am in the midst of my daily ritual of clearing space on the women's bench for myself.

Joshua whispers, "Don't you know you are sowing dissension? You are spoiling the services. You should know woman's place."

I look at him, at his soft black eyes lined lightly with mascara, at his full mouth, at the pains he takes to straighten his hair.

"Joshua," I whisper back, "don't you know that in this place we are both women?"

His gaze shifts quickly to those entering on his side of the curtain, and he withdraws.

Does he think, privately, that they would put him away from them, behind a curtain, on a separate bench, if he proclaimed himself?

Does he wonder if they would forbid his entering this or any house of worship?

The Catholic Church is closed to him.

Fundamentalist Protestantism is closed to him.

So he's here in this naive little synagogue. Joshua is here with his biblical name after the conqueror of Jericho. He's here as the heir of Moses's power. Joshua is here, with his need to exult, to rage, to despair. Protected by men. Totally separated from women.

He is at home with the text, with the call to the Lord, the King of Kings, the Father of Abraham.

Who else would protect him?

New York, Friday, February 27

Dad, I say, a continuation of the news. Robert McFarlane, formerly of the National Security Administration, tells the Tower panel investigating the Iran-Contra affair that "the president clearly didn't understand the nature of the operation, who was involved and what was happening."

My father would have said, You believe that?

I shift often between deep feeling for the liturgy and distraction from it or anger with it.

I watch the men don their prayer shawls, whispering inside the shawls. When the men wrap the phylacteries around their left arms, they are performing a kind of betrothal rite. They whisper privately:

> Thus says the Lord: I will betroth you to Me forever. I will betroth you with righteousness, with justice, with love, and with compassion. I will betroth you to Me with faithfulness, and you shall love the Lord.
>
> (from *A Prayerbook for Shabbat, Festivals, and Weekdays*, ed. Rabbi Jules Harlow [New York: Rabbinical Assembly, United Synagogue of America], p. 7.))

No woman will ever know them as well as the Lord or will have that sense of faithfulness, kindness, or mercy.

I love the legalistic language, the rationality as well as the ecstasy. I am fascinated by the codification.

For instance, there are things that one enjoys in this life and for which one stores up credit in the afterlife: "honoring parents, lovingkindness; attending the house of study . . . morning and evening . . . ; making peace between one person and another, and between man and wife." But, above all, is "the study of Torah" (from *A Prayerbook for Shabbat*, p. 9).

Sometimes I long to be in that kind of world, to be a Yentl. Then I wonder if there is such a world.

As I become sentimental, conversely, I also become rebellious.

Early in the morning's service, when the men say Ah-main to the benedictions, I call out the opposite benediction.

When they praise God, "Who has not made me a woman," I yell out, "Who has not made me a man, *Esh*," while the reader, startled, stops.

"You can't write the script as you go along," says the shammes.

I keep calling out my version, but the *lehner*, the reader, never pays attention and davens right through my words.

Right after services I rush for an appointment with my chiropractor on East Eighty-sixth Street. I take the Lexington subway uptown with difficulty. I cannot turn over in bed. I cannot rise from bed. And when I have risen, I walk stiffly, carefully, as if I have suddenly, permanently aged.

There is a sign on the office door: "Gone due to conference."

Her assistant, with heavy hand and brusque manner, has agreed to see me. After treatment I lift myself off the table and my body once more is in my control.

At the next appointment I ask Cecelia, "What conference?"

"A Vic Damone concert," she laughs.

Usually New Age tapes play in the waiting room, minimalist sounds like a leaking faucet, water on pebbles, faint changes of tone. It's good to know that Vic Damone can also heal.

New York, Saturday, February 28

Bob goes with me to give me courage this Shabbos. We sit in the back row of the main sanctuary. The synagogue had been, until now, Conservative in its practices, with mixed seating in the main sanctuary. Under pressure from Ornstein's crew, however, changes are taking place without the membership's having voted on them.

Women cannot be members. Women do not have a vote. Women *can* join the Sisterhood, put on a *kiddish*, a luncheon, and hold a charity bazaar.

The women's side is supervised by the head of the Sisterhood who, hat atilt, marches up and down the aisle. She shakes her finger at those in close conversation. More importantly, she sees to it that their space is limited. Thus, by enforcing the strictest of rules, *her* space is enlarged.

The membership is aging, attendance thinning, and the synagogue is in real economic trouble and in danger of closing. Yet the rules are getting stricter and driving away potential members.

I am reading the Saturday prayer book, waiting for the four times I say kaddish, rising each time, practicing ahead for the extra-long Kaddish of the Scholars. Although hard for me to say, it is my favorite, originally a blessing on finishing studying, and it honors teachers and teachers of teachers and all who study and let us say Ah-main.

As I am reading, the shadow of the *gabbai*, the man who calls out the page number and does other chores connected with the service, falls over me.

He is a pleasant man, someone to be respected. He was rescued from a concentration camp at the end of World War Two by Allied troops. He immigrated to the States where he became a successful businessman and a generous contributor to the shul. He is white haired and bustling, rushing around to give *aliyah*s, honors, to the men.

We have seen the *gabbai* there every Sabbath. On the anniversary of his rescue from the concentration camp, he sponsored a *kiddish*, an elaborate luncheon in the meeting hall for this elderly, impoverished congregation.

We smile at the *gabbai*, but he is serious.

"You are not allowed to sit together," he says sternly to Bob and me. But he looks at me.

The women have always sat in the main sanctuary wherever they pleased. The more Orthodox women often sat to one side. The men who wished separation sat to the other, and families sat together in the middle. This permissive seating arrangement is anathema to the Trio and Rabbi Ornstein.

"You must sit on the other side," says the *gabbai*, pointing to the narrow aisle of seats flush against the far wall. The head of Sisterhood is standing, awaiting me.

"Since when?" Bob asks.

"Never," I say. "I'll never move."

The *gabbai* tells two women friends sitting together near me that they must henceforth also be moved to the far wall.

Sisterhood is looking to see where she can crowd us in this otherwise sparsely attended synagogue.

"Nothing doing," say the other women.

"Join with them," says Bob.

I want to leave services. I have yet another flashy garment, a snow white polar bear coat. I wrap it around myself haughtily, prepared to march out, like Gloria Swanson making an exit in a silent film.

"Stay," says Bob. "You have support in them."

The rabbi comes out to invite us into a *kiddish*.

"No," I refuse. "I can't be segregated when I pray and integrated when I eat."

I am angry with him. His *dvar Torah*, Torah lesson, in today's sermon, is the sanctity of the synagogue based solely on the *mekhitza*, the separation between men and women.

The rabbi has succumbed to pressure. The Musketeers look very pleased with themselves. And Gray Beard. And Joshua, prancing and carrying the Torah and rushing past the rows of women so none of them can reach out to kiss it. He sees me and the two women and does not even come down our row, though all have crowded to the aisle to greet the parading Torah.

The two women near me are enraged.

"That seat has been my seat since I joined the shul twenty years ago," says Fran, "right after I lost my husband."

Her Hadassah friend, Sarah, is married.

"If my husband can't sit with me, he'll object," says Sarah. "And I will more than object if I can't sit with him during the High Holy Days."

"It's changed," says the sweet-faced blond widow, Fran. "Since these new men came in, they want it all for themselves."

The rabbi gives in. The Trio has met its match in the Hadassah women. Have they forgotten that the women of Hadassah are the most successful of the fund-raising organizations for Israel? That they are the most concerned about health projects and have a hospital in Jerusalem with that name? That their membership is often lifelong?

"Never mind," says the rabbi. "The *gabbai* made a mistake. I'll bawl him out right now."

I am still restless to go, but Bob restrains me.

"Be with them," he says. "You'll make a team."

The women prevail upon us to have a *kiddish* with them. With Fran's scarf and Sarah's purse, they save seats for us at their card table in the meeting hall. They rush for the food before the herd pours in, and then they serve us. "Here's egg salad; here's herring; here's babeganush."

The rabbi also joins us. He is very courtly and makes an impassioned speech.

"I would rather dismiss the minyan," he cries, "than hurt a woman."

Should I believe this, Dad? I ask.

He taught me a necessary cynicism early. I always rigorously assessed the news and its source.

New York, Monday, March 2

The rabbi is only making proclamations. He's in no danger of losing his minyan. Now he has two of them, mine at 7:45 and the early one at 6:45.

Rabbi Ornstein has taken tremendous pleasure planning little breakfasts for those who come early. As I arrive I see them leaving, smacking their lips. So many people have switched that we have more trouble than ever getting our quota. I wonder sometimes about invading their haven, their safe space.

The shammes goes to both minyanim. He's taken to comparing ours to theirs unfavorably.

"Had a fine minyan this morning," he says, "lots of men, and bagels also. And here we can't scratch up ten men or a crumb of bread."

Even Tsibble trains in earlier from Williamsburg for an extra *kiddish*. He comes to our minyan bright eyed from schnapps.

Yet some codaveners, like Fred, have been steadfast, have come up to me to shake my hand and congratulate me on holding my own.

Some have done it with a nod of the head and a significant look, like Larry, the button man.

Others, like Arnold, the sports fan, approach me in the back row of the main sanctuary on Sabbaths to say, "Don't let them bench you."

The rabbi says, "Have courage. Have strength."

P. M.

Often after daily service I go to the Writers' Room, a shared space for writers to work in carrels or small offices. And there I have other rituals.

I change into a sweatsuit to be more athletic when taking on my novel.

I water my plant.

I raise the window a notch and look out at the two brownstones across the street. One is a convent, the other privately rented apartments. Through the window of one I have seen the nuns saying their beads and, through the window of the other, naked men caressing one another.

When I'm in the Writers' Room, I am not at home, not at the synagogue, not on campus, not really in the city. It's the only place where I'm in my own space.

Michele Landsberg, Canadian journalist, is to meet me at Pierre's, a restaurant in the West Village, across the street from my studio.

Michele is late. I wait outside in the cold winter air for her. I contemplate the possibilities for the tardiness: a subway slowdown or a missed stop or a wrong train, all the disasters that befall the city traveler using mass transportation.

I have waited over half an hour and decide to depart. I walk east, toward Sixth Avenue, when down Waverly Place I think I see her curly head riding by in a taxi. I run back. She descends and we embrace. To have almost missed each another!

We talk about a column she wrote for her Toronto newspaper. She has been thinking and rethinking the case of Baby M, whose birth mother is Mary Beth Whitehead and sperm donor, Dr. William Stern.

The court in New Jersey is debating the case, the judge humiliating Mrs. Whitehead at every turn.

Until now, Michele has been favorable to Dr. Stern, thinking he would give the baby a middle-class life. The women's community meets to debate and discuss the issue. Gradually Michele changes her mind.

She shows me her column about to appear:

> What kind of man would make a pitch for public sympathy on the grounds that his relatives died in the Holocaust? I'll answer that. The same man who would marry a Methodist, impregnate a Catholic, pledge to raise the child Unitarian, and then lay claim to the child on the basis of carrying on his heritage.

I invite Michele to address my M.F.A.'s in Westchester in the near future.

She tells the class seated around the conference table:

> I've had to change my mind as an investigative journalist. You have to be able to listen, to be proven

wrong. And, if you are neutral and always even-handed, it means you only support the status quo.

Two of my would-be fiction writers, upon hearing Michele speak of her life and work, change their minds about writing fiction and decide to become journalists.

As I bed down each night, I resolve to continue saying kaddish. I even become hubristic.

I praise myself for rising early, for fulfilling a contract I made between me and my father.

I praise myself for doing this before I train out of the city to teach.

I thought that would be all that would be demanded of me. I am full of self-praise and, immediately after, self-doubt.

The battle, namely, the right to mourn for one's own, is large.

"It's an honorable battle," says Bob.

But what am I doing, sitting alone on a bench?

Everything seems to be a matter of degree. I'm even told that I am one of the fortunate.

An Orthodox acquaintance listens to my complaints unsympathetically.

"You're very lucky," she tells me, "that they even allow you to pray where you are."

"Behind the curtain?"

"Where else?" says the woman.

New York, Tuesday, March 3

It's as if all the bad boys are here today, throwing their spitballs before the rabbi of the shul enters.

The new-coined Jew, Schlomo, says to me, "You're despoiling this place and defaming your father's memory."

"Don't mention my father," I retort. "I won't have his name coming out of your impure mouth."

I'm learning, quite nicely, thank you, to be a holy bitch.

No one says anything to back me up, though I know Fred is desperately thinking of another joke to make me laugh later.

The dear cranky shammes only opens and closes his hand, making a fist and releasing it.

The men have been winding the tefillin seven times around their arms, twining it between their fingers, holding onto the black leather strap. Their attention is engaged.

Only Tsibble sidles up to my bench.

"Shame, shame on their name," he sing-songs.

Ralph, who in only a year has learned to daven so fluently that he is our reader, says nothing but is watching.

At the end of the service, Ralph tells me, "Don't forget why you're here. That's your only purpose."

I see it now. Far in the future, there will be a plaque on this bench: "The only woman to be seated here during the year, thus integrating the services."

Here no man challenges another. Where would these elderly men go for the morning? Who else would make their instant coffee, praise their power when handling some aspect of the Torah reading, count and recount them to make sure there are ten of them, a flock, a flood of them?

Schlomo, in his new costume of Orthodoxy, would roam his room at home.

Ornstein, without his congregation, could preach only to the mirror.

And Joshua, where else would he march regally up and down the aisle, with all the congregants' arms reaching out to touch him, the bearer of the Torah?

The men have been in collusion this morning, affixing the curtain yet farther over the women's bench.

When the rabbi arrives, he looks around and asks me, "Is everything okay?"

I shake my head. He doesn't notice.

The others sit up straight and attentive.

The baleful glances in my direction blur the pages as if I needed new reading glasses.

"We're taking the Concorde this morning," says the rabbi. "A speedy trip to Paris. Everybody ready? Buckle up the seat belts. Take off!"

New York, March

There is emotional whiplash, daily rejection/acceptance, in this little prayer room. Today the men greet me warmly.

"Koosh, koosh," says Tsibble, kissing the back of my hand in a surprisingly courtly gesture.

The rabbi says, "You looked *schvach* yesterday, a little pale, a little weak. I was going to phone if you didn't show up today."

"Don't let it get to you," says Ralph, coming over to my bench and tarrying there.

Yesterday Ralph honored his father's *yahrzeit,* anniversary of his death, like a good son, with twenty friends and a *kiddish.*

That gives me an idea.

I'm a good daughter. Who says I can't bring twenty friends and have a *kiddish?*

Twenty women friends, that is. I will alert the women.

Fred is so glad to see me he tells a joke right away.

When Moses first came down from the mountain he had fifteen commandments.

"Fifteen," said the people, "that's too many. Nobody will obey that many."

So Moses goes up again to bargain with God and comes down.

"I've got good news and bad news," Moses tells the congregated. "I've got it down to ten, but adultery stays in."

I laugh. I don't know exactly why.

Sexual tension continues these mornings in the synagogue. Some of it comes from lack of other occupation. Some from loneliness. Some from reaching out for warmth.

The rabbi calls me *Estherke* and takes my hand. The shammes pinches my cheek in a round circle until I think a hole has been bored through. Every morning Fred kisses me warmly on the mouth when he sees me.

Fred could have his pick among the Sisterhood. And, in his high-rise, he is sought after among the widows.

And yet the death of his wife is a restraint upon him.

This day I spend some time with Fred. He tells me about himself.

"The only story I know is my own," he says, "and the main thing about my life is that it was a schlep. But not always so. I was married to a lovely lady and we were good to each other. She made me laugh when I was cranky. I rubbed her back when she was tired.

"I was in the shoe business, contact man for the factories in Maine and Boston, salesman to the stores in Providence, Rhode Island, and Bridgeport, Connecticut. Without me the Northeast would still be walking barefoot.

"It won't surprise you where we met. In a shoe store. I was trying out a new line. She walked in. What a foot—trim, narrow ankle, high instep, hard to fit, but feet like a queen. Even in the end, when her whole body swoll up, even after her face," he turns away, "didn't look like her face, she kept the same size last, the same width, a trim shoe."

That is a faithful husband.

I think of faith. I keep pondering this. Is my coming here just convenience? Is it that I'm inured by now? Or does the strictness, the stern rules of this place, satisfy something in me? That wildly flailing grief, that accusation when someone's been taken away, has been contained.

This is the seduction of Orthodoxy. And yet I was never easily seduced.

Not even by the jokester.

Leisure World, Sunday, January 18

THE FUNERAL

I did not have the privilege of that last intimate attendance upon my father, *taharah*, the washing of the body. Nor did I select his burial clothes. My brother Jay and Mother selected a silk tie, chose his new blue suit, and, despite his preference for short-sleeved shirts, dressed him this time in a long-sleeved formal shirt. My intimacy with him would be his stories. I would wait upon him in memory.

We gathered at the funeral parlor in the Valley, an hour-and-a-half ride from Leisure World. The cemetery was chosen for its view. We were all there—my brothers, my children, the American relatives, the Russian relatives, and Dad's friends from the retirement community.

Jay had chartered a bus for the retirees who, though well acquainted with death, would find Sunday, the 18th of January, a most difficult day. Services for my father were being held in the Valley in the morning, and in the afternoon, back in Leisure World, another favorite resident of their community was being buried. Trips to and from the funeral would take three hours.

All the data, duties, information relating to death was new to me, and this was a field of their expertise. They had heard many eulogies before. Their lives were becoming elegiac and mine was just one more speech.

Jay told anecdotes, funny and moving, about my father and sports:

Although he was puny, probably through malnourishment in his childhood, and also unathletic, my father loved sports. He thought of sports as the great American pastime. He was even sports editor in his peripatetic early newspaper days.

He had worked in a factory in Detroit and had gone to the city college at the same time. He worked at Packard's Motor Car. When we would tease him about his lack of mechanical ability, he would say, "What do you mean I'm not mechanical? I can install the cotter pin in a 1922 Packard."

He saved enough money to be able to attend the University of Michigan in Ann Arbor. He worked as a dishwasher at hospitals, and he would sell his comp tickets to the sport events. He stood outside the stadium and heard the crowds roar, and he could never attend a game.

In his last years the games were his joy, his extravagance. When the U of M band struck up the Wolverines' song, "Hail to the Victor Valiant," he would rise and place his hand over his heart.

He and I have gone to the Rose Bowl together, waving U of M banners and cheering on the Wolverines.

I tell family stories, newspaper stories, Leisure World stories. The funeral director looks around, surprised to see the mourning party laughing heartily.

I end my remarks with what is said at the end of the funeral service, *Titzchak l'yom acharon.* He will laugh until the final day.

"Go, Daddy," I say, "make God laugh. Perhaps God needs it more than we."

℟

New York, March

A.M.

The sexton bawls me out seriously today.

"This keddusha is the holiest of prayers. You've been coming long enough to know that. And look at your posture, one foot in front of the other, slouching.

"Stand like a soldier, Madam. You're facing the Almighty."

"Shammes," says the rabbi, "not so rough."

"No," I say, "he honored me, first of all, by observing me and, secondly, by correcting me."

Dad, I say, David Daniel Kaminsky died this week.
My father would have replied, You can't fool me. That's Danny Kaye.

P.M.

Bob and I are on the board of a theater company.
I have begun to fancy that my life is a play.
"Not commercial enough," says Bob.
There is a fund-raiser and the trustees are invited. Bob and I arrive at this elegant apartment on the East Side and look around. Nobody looks back.
A man smoking a cigar in the close room comes up to introduce himself to us.
"What do you do?" he asks the both of us.
We don't do stocks or real estate, as the other trustees "do."
"Bob's a wonderful artist," I say.
"Esther's a marvelous writer," says Bob.
"What kind of writing?" Cigar turns to me.
"Novels, plays . . . ," I begin.
"Forget novels," he says. "What kind of plays?"
I describe the plays being developed for the Deborah Project.
He waves his hand. I think he's waving away the cigar smoke, but he's dismissing me.
"Esther's having an interesting experience now," says Bob, "and she's writing about it."
Then Bob tells Cigar about the shul.
The man actually takes the cigar out of his mouth.
"I want it," he says. "I'm a famous producer. Write it and I'll get it put on. It could be the stuff legends are made of."

We leave the gathering so distracted that we press the button for the service elevator and take it down to the street. We are also the only guests to subway home. Limousines are awaiting the others.

We are starry eyed, dreaming about Broadway.

"But, Bob," I ask, "have you ever heard of this famous producer?"

But then, what do we know?

New York, March

Bob and I are swimming the lanes at the Y.

I swim and compose. I turn the shul into a commercial play. All it needs is romance.

I breaststroke, backstroke, and dream it up:

The rabbi will peer behind the *mekhitza* and fall in love with the "lady." She will also be attracted to him. He is a widower whose little children go to the Sunday school. She watches them on Sunday. She sees him hugging them tenderly. She hears them giggling.

That first day, the rabbi approaches the woman and asks, "How is it going here for you?"

"Not so good," says the woman. "They don't appreciate me. They call me half-a-man."

"You're all woman to me," says the rabbi.

The rabbi arranges for a matchmaker to formally introduce them.

Once chaperoned, they sit and talk. They have much in common. He is lonely. She in her forties has longed for a family.

"Would you do one little thing for me, my dear?" he asks sweetly.

"What?"

"Shave your head."

I tell Bob as we swim back and forth in neighboring lanes.

"It could even be a musical," I say. "What rhymes with *mekhitza?*"

"Pizza," says Bob.

I am laughing so hard I swallow water.

"Forget it," Bob shakes his head.

I should forget what the famous producer said, "This is the stuff legends are made of"?

New York, March

I phone my mother and tell her about Cigar and my "legendary" play.

"Dad on Broadway!" says Mom. "We'll all charter a flight from Leisure World, Nate and Isidore and Mike."

"Wait a bit," I say.

"In the meantime," says my mother, "I'll look around for something to wear at the premiere."

New York, March

The most terrible thing happened in shul.

It was a dreadful, snowy, blowy day. My feet were soaked by the time I reached the synagogue. Services had just started when there was a disturbance in the hall.

One of the young men went out to see what was happening. The rabbi followed.

A black man's voice could be heard:

"I'm sorry to disturb you, Rabbi. I respect your synagogue. I'm a Vietnam War veteran, and I can't get a job for fifty cents an hour shoveling snow. I'm hungry, Rabbi."

The rabbi gave the veteran some money and sent him back out into the street.

"This is only a place of words," I told the rabbi, "not of spirit."

I went to the front doors of the synagogue and stood there in the cold looking for the Vietnam veteran. The street was full of what looked like Vietnam vets seeking food and shelter.

I returned chilled.

The shammes is telling a story.

"I went to my doctor for my annual checkup.

" 'How'm I doing, Doc?' I ask him.

" 'A-OK,' he tells me.

" 'So when should I return, Doctor?' I ask.

" 'Next year,' says the doctor, 'for your annual checkup.' "

The shammes cackles.

"May you live until you're a hundred and twenty," says the rabbi.

"Who are you to limit my years?" laughs the shammes.

I begin collecting anecdotes. I am also composing a letter inviting my women friends to meet the "characters" of this place.

Leisure World, Early January

This last visit to my father is spent walking and talking. I learn about my parents' lives and worries in Leisure World.

"Why has the electric bill become so large?" Mom asks.

"What about the bill for my hearing aid?" Dad asks. "How much am I medically covered for?"

I see our Chanukah present to him, David Shipler's book, *Enemies in the Promised Land,* about Arabs and Jews living in Israel, has a bookmark. Dad always read a book nonstop. I realize this is a hard book for him, enmity in Israel.

"We take out books from the bank," says Dad. "Banks are our new libraries."

"Why is that?" Bob asks.

"Well," says Dad, "there are more banks per square mile in Leisure World than in any other section of the country."

"They have to compete," says Mom. "Some give dance lessons. That was the bank we didn't choose. But the bank that offered free luncheons, to that I go. The bank also invited our whole Hadassah chapter to lunch."

"The more intellectual banks," smiles Dad, "have libraries. The only trouble is, more people deposit money than take out books."

New York, Friday, March 6

At shul this morning the guys and I talk about headlines and news events while we discard our winter
wear. No one here has read or is interested in the Baby
M case. Not only is the trial held in New Jersey but it
is too removed from their daily travails. What touches
them is the news from Israel, synagogue politics, and
the cost of living in New York.

Marilyn French has given me a petition for which to
gather signatures from women for the Baby M case:

> According to the standards being applied in the
> Baby M custody case, we are all unfit mothers. We
> color our hair, we can't play patty-cake right, our
> husbands drink, our in-laws fight, we have too many
> pandas and not enough pots for our kids to play
> with, we're broke, we tend to get excited and emo-
> tional. . . . We who have signed this statement want
> to urge legislators and courts to recognize that a
> mother need not be perfect to deserve her children.

Much of what is important to me has no impact
whatsoever on my co-congregants.

The last two days we started late at the synagogue.

I sat in this crowded space, benched and closeted.
We waited a long time for minyans the past two days.
Today again the rabbi and the Professor are both late.

Yesterday they came in, the Professor's arm in a
sling. He had fallen and wrenched his shoulder and
broken his arm.

The Professor is a stern man, a martinet, a Distinguished Professor Emeritus. He is the one who flicks

his tallis at me, who averts his eyes from direct gaze with mine. Yet, when Rabbi Ornstein had one of his explosions, this Professor said, "Two wrongs do not make a right."

Tsibble is in the corridor today. I hear him asking in Yiddish if the Professor hurts. I step into the rabbi's office to see the Professor. He is sitting there, shoelaces dangling. I bend to tie his laces.

"No!" he says.

I ignore his objections and begin to retie his laces.

"So you won't trip," I say.

I am crouched there when I suddenly feel his hand upon my head. I look up, surprised. He has avoided glance and touch these weeks.

"Thank you," he says, his eyes full of tears.

"We're here for each other," I tell him.

I help him off with his coat and rush back for kaddish. He is so pathetic, alone and helpless.

This little *shtiebl*, this room, is full of lonely, elderly widowers or single men, their days stretching emptily before them.

Fred says, "I'm thinking of going to the Ninety-second Street Y to join a bridge club. That's one thing I could do, play a nice game of bridge. Also," he says, "I play a nice game of Ping-Pong."

Is he hinting that I be a bridge, Ping-Pong, or any other kind of partner?

But Fred, on whom we all count to be cheerful, is looking wan.

His health has been impaired since World War Two, when he was wounded while serving in the Navy. All he has told me is that he was in a veteran's hospital for over a year as a result of his wounds. I worry when he misses a day and phone him in the evening.

"I'm here, Princess," he says, "just playing hooky."

But something hurts him. There is an unhealed wound.

Larry, the button man, approaches me.

"Could you help me?" he asks.

His hands are arthritic. His cuffs have become unbuttoned. I button them.

"You're a good girl," he says.

Arnold always sits by himself, surrounded by the sports pages of the dailies as well as *Sports Illustrated*.

"What's the news?" I ask him.

"Nothing that would interest you," he says. "No front-page items here."

"My dad loved the front page," I tell Arnold. "In fact, he used to make up the front page."

Arnold puts down *Sports Illustrated*.

"You're a classy, front-page lady," he says and returns to the magazine.

"Missus! Missus!" It's Tsibble. "How is it by you?" he asks.

"Very well, and by yourself?"

He grins. His teeth are various shades: white, gold, brown stained.

"I like you, Missus," says Tsibble.

I am suddenly beginning to feel like Sister Kenny.

Mary Gordon says, after she's been particularly attentive and polite to a group of demanding people, "I'm wearing my Sister Kenny white shoes."

P.M.

I am emboldened by my day to plan an action and request help from my friends. I send off a group letter:

3/6/87

Dear Minyan Mates:
As most of you know, I have been saying kaddish for my father for six weeks. It's been an education for

all of us here, for me who am counted or discounted as half-a-man, and for the others who thought they were safe on an island of males.

I now need you, my sisters. I wish to have a minyan of women to attend the morning service, Sunday, March 29th.

We have accommodated to one another to some extent, I and the ten men, but I want them to know that where I stand, a shadow extends. Now that they can almost recognize me, I also want them to realize we women WILL invade and WILL honor our dead.

The women I have selected will be surprised to get this letter, and the rabbi will be surprised when I inform him that I, like Ralph, am honoring my father. I will have a *kiddish* afterward also.

I begin to dream that soon all barriers are down and the *mekhitza* is thrown into the garbage.

Something does happen. But not exactly that.

New York, Sunday, March 8

Morning minyan. One short.

A father and his young son have come for some weeks now on Sundays. The shammes asks how old the boy is and if he is a bar miztvah.

"Not yet," says the father. "But shortly."

"So count him, then," says the shammes.

I, at the other end of the room, am not counted though long past the age of covenant.

Dad, I say, I remember your story.

Dad used to tell us about his favorite teacher in the Milwaukee schools, either an English or history teacher, for Dad excelled at both subjects. Dad remembered how knowledgeable and stimulating she was.

"She used to advise the school janitor how to vote," said my father, "because it was before suffrage and she herself wasn't allowed to vote."

In the House of Hope, it's before suffrage.

But I am taking a postsuffrage action.

I grin and think about my dad and remember listening, late at night, to Dad's typing. I remember watching him write columns for his labor newspaper or for a Jewish-English weekly that he edited or for a neighborhood newspaper that he put out in two hours. His tongue stuck out between his teeth when he concentrated. He typed, two fingers on each hand flying. And I thought that click-clack, that setting in order of words, was a melody I could play. Neither of us could carry a tune, but we could carry a story.

ℵ

New York, Tuesday, March 10

The rabbi decides to hold the second minyan at 7:35, ten minutes earlier, in the hopes of attracting more "customers," as he puts it.

It was over seventy degrees in the city yesterday—exceptionally warm for March. My friend Rose drove us to Brighton Beach to sit on the sand, look at the waves, and watch the parade of Russians on the boardwalk, *spatzlering* arm in arm, the heavy, befurred women with beehive hairdos and their broad-chested men.

Today it is bitter cold.

This morning I enter the synagogue to find an old, stooped-over man spreading his belongings along my bench. I am confused.

Do I use this as an opportunity to sit on the men's side? Do I decide to sit with a man on this bench behind the *mekhitza*?

I begin moving his things, his coat, his tallis bag. He stands up swinging, flailing his arms at me.

"She's a thief! The lady's a thief! She stole my tallis bag."

There is silence.

Tsibble begins singing, "*Ganev, ganev. Fonya is a ganev.*"

It seems this song character, Fonya, steals borscht and kasha. And I'm stealing a tallis bag.

The reader this morning is Ralph. He turns around, amused.

Fred, my joker friend, says to this stranger, "You're in her place."

I feel funny. Am I Queen of the Bench? On the other hand, I don't want to sit with this schmuck.

Ralph laughs loudly and says, "What an irony. Saved by the *mekhitza.*"

"Nuts," says Fred. "We're all kinds of nuts in here."

"What's going on?" Schlomo from the earlier minyan sticks his head in.

"I'm just talking about nuts," says Fred. "Filberts, walnuts, hazelnuts, peanuts, almonds, coconuts, chestnuts. Join us if you fit in."

The rabbi says, "Speedily, speedily, gentlemen, the last play of the final inning. Bat the ball over the fence and we're out of here."

P. M.

A surprise birthday party for Bob.

Bob has been commuting from Detroit to New York twice a week for four years (as have I), teaching in both cities. His art has consisted of monoprints and paintings of airplane scenes: the euphemism of instruction on airplane cards, the planes that were forced to land in water and are floating like beached whales, the passengers assuming the crash position.

This theme of crash and near-miss consumes his work. He arrives at his destination pleasantly enough, but it must be nightmarish for him in flight. I know of no other artist who uses this subject matter.

So it is not surprising that the guests have brought airplane motif gifts: an airplane chocolate mousse cake with a plastic airplane and icing, like skywriting: "Keep Flying, Bob." There are paper airplane cutouts, children's airplane books, airplane cards.

From Rose, Bob gets a soft woolen scarf with airplanes woven into the material. Linsey Abrams, my colleague, and Ann Volkes bring Bob a T-shirt with imprinted instructions on what to do in case of a crash.

It is a fine, laughing party, and Bob smiles in his new year gracefully.

New York, Wednesday, March 11

After davening, the rabbi and I sit on my bench (now it's *my* bench) while he explicates text.

He is speaking of the two times the Ten Commandments are referred to in the Torah and the subtle differences that appear in the version in Deuteronomy (in Hebrew, *Dvarim*, meaning "words," from the opening of the section, "These are the words which Moses spoke").

The rabbi says that the commandment, when first stated in Exodus, reads, "Honor thy mother and father that their days may be long in the land." The second time, to the original commandment is added, "and it should go well with you."

The rabbi is really complimenting me by choosing the commandment of honoring one's parents.

I then tell the rabbi about my women's minyan coming up at the end of the month.

"It's not a proper minyan," he says and then tries to figure out how closely we can sit on this narrow bench, all of us behind the *mekhitza*.

The rabbi and Fred come to Bob's and my loft for coffee.

Bob is very generous. He removes a beautiful color etching from his cabinet, *How Goodly Are Thy Tents,* a saying from the beginning of services, and donates it to the synagogue.

The rabbi, smiling, accepts.

"It's not for them," he decides, "it's for me. And I know a place where I can have it framed for a bargain."

He knows all the bargains—clothing, food, or electronics. In the rabbi himself the synagogue has a bargain—a one-man band, rabbi, cantor, teacher, spiritual bookkeeper. He works six days a week, sometimes seven. Unlike God, he never seems to rest.

New York, Thursday, March 12

I look around the davening room and think of a minyan of my women friends here.

This morning I rise to say the kaddish.

The martinet who used to flick his tallis at me comes to my side of the room. He had always kept strictly to the other side.

The shammes rushes through the kaddish, though I take longer than the others. The Professor waits and gives me the Amen, nodding, reinforcing my prayer.

When I finish, Fred says, "You're getting along real good with your Hebrew."

The shammes grins at me, "You're better with aging."

Arnold lingers on his way to his law office to tell a sports story. He jokes with Fred, who has been absent with stomach flu.

"Watch it," Arnold warns Fred. "You'll be replaced. You know the story of Wally Pipp of the New York Yankees, don't you? It was about 1921 and Wally Pipp, their first baseman, got up with a terrible stomachache. Just like you, Fred. Pipp asked the manager if he could sit out that game.

" 'Sure, Wally,' said the manager, and he replaced Wally Pipp with Lou Gehrig, the best first baseman the Yankees ever had, and Gehrig played that position for twenty years. So, watch it, Fred, no stomachache or you'll be replaced in the minyan."

"Some threat!" laughs Fred.

We are flying to California to help Mother select a plaque for Dad's grave.

I will be absent. Will they replace me?

Eden Memorial Park, California, Tuesday, March 17

We—my mother, brother Jay, Bob, and I—go to Eden Memorial Park to choose the plaque.

We are ushered into the office of a salesman whose walls are covered with pacesetter certificates, with awards that send him to Maui and to Mexico.

This Pacesetter, who can hardly pause when we ask questions, keeps running out and slamming the heavy door on us. He is utterly insensitive to the situation. We don't let it faze us. We discuss type and color of plaque—bronze or granite and, as for granite, gray or brownish stone.

We discuss design: eternal flame, thorny rose, opened book.

The plaque is already paid for on the plan my parents arranged, but, at the funeral, this same Pacesetter told my mother she would have to pay an additional amount.

"A *ganev*, a thief," my mother says.

Today, suspicious of him, she has armed herself with her contract showing she paid in full. We make some changes in the set patterns shown us, and the Pacesetter tells us it will cost more.

In the meantime, his clerk in the office checks with the monument makers and discovers it will not cost a penny more. He is annoyed with her for saying this in our presence, while Mother grins, waving her contract under the Pacesetter's nose or fanning herself with it, which distracts him as he speaks.

We choose the design of the opened book and, across it, Jay's phrase, "From his pen to God's ear." Then Jay is carried away by the metaphor. When the rest of us leave, he will do variations. For Mother, "From her kitchen to God's nose." For Bob, "From his paintbrush to God's eye."

The salesman is unamused.

The salesman tells us that we can't have *God* on the plaque, for the plaques are inlaid on the graves and a tractor–lawn mower rolls over them.

"Do you want the name of God mown?" asks the Pacesetter.

"How about *HaShem*?" Jay asks, an appellation, "The Name" (of God).

"We could have trouble," says the salesman grumpily. "I'll let you know."

He accompanies us to Dad's plot. We become somber as we approach. Mother, so restrained always, weeps quietly.

The Pacesetter keeps talking.

"The stone is only a marking. These could just be numbers. Your father could be 38F. It's nothing. We're dust to dust."

He leaves us there while he gets in his car, his overly padded shoulders squarish behind the wheel.

"With you guys around, I didn't set any paces today," he calls back.

We watch him leave in a cloud of dust. We're so angry we laugh.

"How does a mortician sign a letter?" jokes Jay. "Eventually yours."

Leisure World, Thursday, March 19

I remember standing in Eden Memorial Park at my father's plot. I think how little room he takes up, a bird curled inward, or something carapaced that has shed its skin.

Has he started to decompose, or is he still composed, yarmulke on his head, hands on his breast, tallis creamy white, false teeth in place, his face serene?

My mother's chest pains are more frequent. She is frightened at night when they come, so she sleeps on three pillows, has her nitroglycerin pill on her table, and her doctor-son's phone number at hand. She cannot catch her breath.

I say, "Be well. Hold on. I'll be coming back to speak for your temple. Just be there."

She shakes her head. "I can't promise."

"Not even for my speech?" I ask.

She looks up tiredly, then mischievously, "It better be a *very* good speech."

New York, Friday, March 20

Friday. Back from California.

The fifth *mekhitza*, a gaudy piece of material with large lace flowers, was caught up on the pole, put up there by the earlier minyan. I arrive and do not disturb it. Let it be wound up in the air.

Schlomo unwinds the curtain. It hangs to the floor, obscuring not only my head and body but even my shoes.

"As the rabbi would wish," he states.

"Are you the Keeper of the Rag?" I ask him.

Just then, the rabbi appears.

"I'll be gone a week," he says to Schlomo, "and I expect you to keep them from bothering her with the *mekhitza*."

He's placed me in the hands of the enemy! I better get a Women's Minyan here in a hurry.

The rabbi, I discover, is going to a Hasidic tennis hotel in Miami.

I say, "I didn't know there was such a thing."

"Why not?" asks the rabbi. "As for myself, I'm a champion player."

With tallis around his shoulder, prayer book in one hand, yarmulke on his head, he pretends to swing the racquet and serve the ball.

After services, I go for my own exercise.

I am in the pool at the Y for my half hour, and as I leave the little children are coming up the stairs for their lesson. They will pass up the ladder of nautical accomplishment from Tadpole to Guppy to Minnow and then Fish and, finally, Flying Fish.

Ahead of me, going down the stairs from the women's locker room, is a peppy young woman who is holding onto the railing as she descends. Her way is blocked by a swimming teacher and her young class.

"Children!" exclaims the young woman. "Is it time for their lesson?"

She feels for the doorknob and briskly enters the exercise room. She is blind.

New York, March 21, Sabbath and Vernal Equinox

My shammes looks subdued. The synagogue is deserted this morning. The rabbi is off to tennis.

"There's nobody here because of the *kiddish*," says Fred. "It's advertised on the bulletin board outside: 'The Men's Club Sponsors the Kiddish.' The members contribute a dollar apiece and, for that, you get no bagels, no herring, no lox, and no attendance."

On the rabbi's high throne chair on the *bima*, the ritual stage, is sitting Ornstein, my antagonist.

His singing is lackluster. He carries the Torah around the synagogue without once looking up or pausing before me.

My Hadassah friends at shul, Fran and Sarah, comment on the substitute.

"He's a newcomer," says Fran. "First time he substituted for Rabbi, he looks at me and delivers a sermon *against* me. I've come with my purse, which contains my glasses and medicines. He talks about my being a *more-*

det, a woman who goes against custom, by carrying on the Sabbath. That's not bad enough. He stares at me while he's talking in case anyone missed the point."

Sarah has just returned from a Hadassah trip to Israel. The country, plagued by bad publicity and falling tourism, welcomes the two thousand members, who spend lavishly. Shimon Peres and the president address them; waiters serve them speedily; entertainers dance for them enthusiastically.

"I had Sarah's schedule with me," says Fran fondly, "and looked on it every day, so I knew exactly where she was and what she was doing."

I sit next to an elderly man, Rafe, in the main sanctuary.

"Two things they ask you when you die," Rafe informs me, "your name and whether you did mitzvahs, good deeds. If you've done no mitzvahs, you suffer."

Rafe looks at Fred the joker, silver haired and laughing.

"He's going to get in trouble when it's his turn to go Up There," says Rafe. "All he'll be able to tell them is his name."

Near the last row of the main sanctuary, where Bob and I sit, the elderly Orthodox men turn from their bench to me and wait as I struggle with my kaddish. I finish long after the sexton.

Ornstein, the substitute rabbi on the *bima,* turns his back on me while I am still standing up with my prayer book.

But my seat companions, Fred, Rafe, and the kindly others, give me an Amen to pin down the kaddish and not let it fly away.

P.M.

I am self-conscious, writing about my mourning experience, anxious whether I am exploiting both the scene and my own pain as I recount the shul tales day after day.

Friends are invited for dinner. Has the synagogue become just after-dinner conversation?

My friend and colleague from Wayne State, Julie Jensen, comes floating in from cocktails with her agent and a producer. They want to take her award-winning play, which was performed at the Arena in D.C., to the Long Wharf in Connecticut.

"New York talk," says Julie. "Promises and names. Who knows what's real about it?"

I show her a letter from Cigar. He loves the first scenes I have sent him.

"I have produced Miller and Williams," he says. "I know what theater is about. It's about this."

Is this New York talk? Is this for real?

A filmmaker from Canada also came over last night. She wants to make a film of my novel *A Weave of Women*. Is this Canadian talk?

We have other guests, a historian, Kathryn Kish Sklar, and her daughter, Susan Sklar Freedman, a film editor. We speak of completed work, Susan's two new films, *Witness to Apartheid*, about the detained children in South Africa, and *Sweet Lorraine*, about a kosher hotel in the Catskills that has to close its doors. They do not sound like equal tragedies, but we all promise to go to the movie house and applaud, especially the credit line for editor.

I tell the dinner guests that I only want to write the novel for which I was given a grant, do Cigar's play, and maybe write the screenplay for the Canadian producer. Is that too much to ask? Will someone give me an Amen?

They do, loudly and soundly.

Then I tell my visitors—the playwright, historian, film editor, filmmaker—about an action I'm planning at the synagogue. So many women will come, I tell my guests, that we won't all fit behind the curtain or on the woman's side, so many that we encroach upon the room, so many that we cast a large shadow.

Again, they give me a rousing Amen.

New York, Mid-March

One of the organizers from the Women's Lobby in Jerusalem has phoned. That's three times this week that we've spoken from such great distance. Figuring out when to reach someone, for Israel is seven hours ahead of New York, is difficult. But the organizer has an even more difficult role for me to play. She is one of those involved in the First International Women Writers' Conference. The organizer believes I am in a unique position to raise funds from Abby Rockefeller so that women authors from all over the world can meet in Jerusalem.

"Why am I in a unique position?"

"You're in the States."

"I don't know Abby Rockefeller," I say.

"That doesn't matter," says the Women's Lobby. "She gives to good causes."

"I don't know where she lives," I say.

But the lobby, far away in Jerusalem, knows where she lives.

"We need her!" insists the organizer. "Don't you want this conference to take place?"

New York, Sunday, March 22

Outside every door in an Orthodox home is a mezuzah, which one kisses upon entering or leaving the room. The little prayer room at *Beit Hatikva* has upon its doorpost the mezuzah, a small container that holds a parchment upon which Deuteronomy 6:4–9 is hand-calligraphied. These words are instructions and commands that should be taught to one's sons, recited morning and night, and bound (with phylacteries) upon the hand, the forehead, and, with the mezuzah, upon one's doorposts.

Only some of the congregants observe the custom of touching the mezuzah. Others come and go at ease.

But this morning an Orthodox young woman joined me on my bench. Her skin was rosy, her dress modest. Upon entering the room she kissed the mezuzah, then rushed to pull the curtain across the women's bench. I stood to the side as usual or sat on a chair next to the bench outside of the curtain. This young woman stood during the whole service while davening, eyes closed, swaying, ecstatic.

The men didn't see her at all, were unaware of her, for she was doing what she was supposed to be doing, lovely and young though she was, while I, this older woman, was still stubbornly in plain view.

The woman davener looked at me in disapproval as she left the room, kissing once again the mezuzah with its rolled information to be passed on to one's son.

Sunday's service is always a disappointment, with people I don't know from my regular days and usually a reader who can only manage a monotone. I begin to get nervous about the 29th, the Sunday of my action.

New York, Monday, March 23

My regular *boychiks*. The Professor rushes over to ask me about my mother's health. I look across the room, the sun bright, the morning about forty-six degrees, and think that I really love about half a dozen men in this room.

Larry stands near me for help in buttoning his cuffs.

"The palsy's worse today," he says. "I can feel it."

I tell him, "It's probably just because of the weather."

"The age," says Larry. "I'm old furniture. I try to play chess, the pieces fall off the board. I try to play checkers because they're easier to handle, I knock them off also. Buttons, forget it. Everything's unfastening."

"Just a little dropsy," I say, and rebutton his cuff. "Take care of yourself."

Arnold is pretending to read the paper but is watching us.

"Arnold," I ask him after Larry has gone off, "why do you hang around here? You're not so religious. You're not in mourning."

And Arnold says, "Here in the A.M., I forget the *tsuris*, the trouble, a man can get himself into."

Without thinking, he sits down next to me on my bench.

"Simplify, that's my rule. Shake it off. Divorce. Custody. But here I'm a valuable member of the team. Here, I'm like Babe Ruth pointing to the spot where he's going to hit the homer during the World Series. And then hitting it there!

"Whatever I do here, I get accolades. I'm not so learned. I say the blessing before they read from the

Torah, they shake my hand. I open the ark, they shake my hand. Here I count. They couldn't manage without me. I'm Hank Greenberg asking special dispensation from the rabbis so he could play for the Detroit Tigers during the High Holy Days."

I am learning new things every day.

"I look out the window while they daven," says Arnold. "I see the ball soaring over the stadium. And I forget. It doesn't even cross my mind for forty whole minutes that I'm just a hack lawyer in small claims court."

My eyes fill with tears as he moves away.

The shammes comes up. He is preening.

"You didn't even mention the change."

"Remind me and I'll mention," I say.

"My lace-up shoes instead of old loafers, my suit, everything matching. The frames of my glasses fixed, no pin holding the arm piece in place. And, unlike Rodney lisping over there, my uppers and lowers in place. Come watch me chomp my way through a bagel."

Tsibble is whistling. Fred is teasing him. Larry, the reader today, knowing how much I enjoy his voice, really lets it ring out. Arnold is reluctantly putting away the sports page. It's like going to camp and loving your bunk mates. How can I ever explain this to my feminist circle?

Then Larry, as reader, reacting to Fred's teasing to speed up the kaddish, says it so fast I stumble trying to keep up. When the men begin punching him in the shoulder to slow down, he slows down, articulating each syllable.

"*Schnell, schnell!*" Tsibble yells.

Larry will not let them flummox him, as he calls it.

Larry and Fred invite me to join the retirees afterward for coffee. That's instant in a styrofoam cup. The

Professor joins us, in great pain with his arm, which still hangs in the sling.

"I wanted to tell you, Madam," he says in his formal way, "that what Ornstein did when he attacked you was wrong and we talked about it afterwards and we all felt badly for you. And we want you to know how welcome, even liked, even well-liked you are, and that after your time of kaddish, we hope you continue to join us."

Even typing this now I am full of emotion.

"It used to be a good group we had here," says Fred, "wonderful guys, wonderful *kiddish* after the service. We laughed and told jokes and I never wanted to go home. It's changed."

At home he sits alone and reads mysteries. He goes to the library every day that it's open.

"I've got a good library book to lend you," Fred says, "about a Jewish detective on the upper West Side. What could be bad about such a combination?"

Arnold is studying the sports section, dawdling before training downtown.

"Who you betting on?" he asks Fred, whatever the sports season: football, basketball, hockey, baseball.

"If I followed your suggestions," says Fred, "I'd be like Tsibble there."

Tsibble hears his name and grins.

Arnold looks at Tsibble. "Tsibble has nothing on me," he says.

We all laugh. He's serious, we later discover.

Am I getting sentimental about my compatriots?

Lest my right hand, O Jerusalem, forget its cunning, let me not forget that I was the only one in the room this morning not attending, in some fashion, to the Torah. They even brought up a nice young man, a Cohen of the priestly cast, and had him daven, even though he didn't know any Hebrew.

"Follow me," said Fred. "I still remember a little from my bar mitzvah, and that was sixty years ago."

The visitor shook hands all around, and the fellows told him, "*Y'yasher ko-akh.*"

But I am without power, never to hear those words from man to man. Don't let me soften too much.

New York, March

Despite all the routines and jokes and kidding around, our minyan has a harder and harder time in getting ten, while the earlier minyan gets twenty and more and has coffee afterward.

The men speak of that other minyan longingly. It's too early for our regulars. Among our regulars are the very elderly. It turns out that our sexton, at ninety-five, was until recently the youngest of a trio. There is Rodney, ninety-seven, who speaks with an empty mouth, a toothless spray. Fred tells me that Rodney was spry until very recently. Indeed, only yesterday he was climbing up on the back of the benches to open a window.

Fred reminisces about the oldest of the three, a gentleman, ninety-nine.

"He was very modern, a delightful fellow. He used to be a liberal, too, would argue against the fanatics who insisted that the two elderly sisters who mourned for their father hide behind the *mekhitza.*"

Fred pauses. "He was mugged," says Fred, "and after that he faded. Who would do that to such an elderly gentleman?"

I think of these ninety-some-year-olds, who in that overheated, airless room—provided there are no muggings or misfortune—live forever. Is it religion or the regular attendance, a schedule, and gainful employment? For instance, toothless Rodney passes the charity box every morning. That's his responsibility and keeps him going. He smiles when I fold a dollar bill and press it through the opening.

"My best customer," he lisps.

He's never been absent all the time I've come.

Our shammes, cranky, shaking his cane, is walking less steadily. I help him down the stairs, and in his impatient rush he puts his cane ahead of him, off the stair, and leans on it. If I had not been holding onto his arm, he would have slid down the whole flight.

I am preparing for the action of the Women's Minyan as well as for the PEN Women's Committee.

I am as impatient as the rabbi this morning.

"*Schnell*," he says. "Let's finish like the New York Marathon in the final stretch up Fifty-seventh Street and Central Park."

The rabbi pulls me aside to ask how my mourning is going.

He has given me a present, Maurice Lamm's *The Jewish Way in Death and Mourning*, with a table of contents from "The Moment of Death" to, at last, "The World Beyond the Grave."

"Did you read about resurrection?" asks the rabbi.

He turns the pages and quotes from Ezekiel 37: "Dry bones . . . [and] there was a noise, and behold a commotion, and the bones came together, bone to its bone . . . and the breath came into them, and they lived, and stood up upon their feet."

"We're not so big on that," I tell him.

"On what?" he asks. "We're speaking of being under the wings of God."

"We're not big on heaven and its feathered creatures," I say.

"So what did you come here for?" he asks.

"Just to mourn," I say.

The rabbi says, "But there has to be something else. If there's nothing there, after all, why should we bother remembering and mourning?"

Don't you think I wonder all the time?

He changes the subject.

"About the *kiddish* to honor your beloved father," the rabbi begins.

"Yes."

"In his blessed memory, how about adding a sheet of lox? I know they rob you blind for lox, but there would be so much excitement that I would put it up on the bulletin board, 'Service. Kiddish with lox.'"

"A sheet of lox it is," I say.

New York, Friday, March 27

I am in the midst of a crushing schedule. I am planning "the *kiddish* with lox," a party with drama, a trip abroad, and a meeting for a writers' organization.

I have a fine houseguest, Naomi Newman of the Traveling Jewish Theatre of San Francisco. We are planning drama in the loft. That will be tonight, Friday night. Sunday, the 29th of March, is the women's action at shul. And in the afternoon I fly off, with Mary Gordon, to the First International Women Writers' Conference in Jerusalem.

The Women's Lobby in Jerusalem wants me to create a closing ritual. What will women from forty countries have in common, and how can I unite them, elevate them, or just give them simple pleasure?

In shul, Fred says, "I've got a joke."
Schlomo says, "The man *is* a joke."
Fred says, "Hear me out."

There are these three guys shipwrecked on a desert island.

One's a Jew, two are non-Jews. The Jew lies down, takes in the sun, while the Protestant and Catholic are scurrying about, trying to get enough brushwood for a fire, trying to signal the ships at sea. All the time, this Jew is on his back, taking it all in.

"What's the matter with you?" asks the Protestant.

"Aren't you worried?" asks the Catholic.

"Let me tell you gentlemen something," says the Jew. "I was in business. First year I made two grand, and I gave the United Jewish Appeal two hundred dollars. I built the business, and soon I made twenty grand and I gave the UJA two thousand. I made two hundred grand later and gave the UJA twenty thousand. Last year I made two million. Don't worry, gentlemen. The UJA's gonna find me."

"See, I'm laughing," says Schlomo, the retread, sarcastically.

We have a new regular in the minyan, an actor who plays character roles. He is wonderfully welcomed.

"How did you come to this synagogue?" I ask him about this modest place.

The actor is dark haired, wears glasses, is not theatrical yet has a commanding presence. I do not yet know that he will be fighting for a leading role at the synagogue.

"I heard the gruff voice of the sexton," he says, "telling me, 'We need you inside for a minyan.' His cranky tone sounded like my father, so I went in and I found that it was nonthreatening, a place where I could daven, where I could learn again what I knew when I was a bar mitzvah."

The actor has set an interesting task for himself. He is relearning his bar mitzvah for his fortieth birthday.

"I'm photocopying my old bar mitzvah pictures for the invitation," says the actor. "There is a photo of my first bar mitzvah and a recent photo. The lettering reads: 'When a boy is bar mitzvah'd, he becomes a man. When a man is bar mitzvah'd, he becomes a giant.'"

Our rabbi has recorded a tape for the actor, who jogs with his *haftorah,* his commentary on the Torah portion, sung into his ears.

He has taken to criticizing me also.

"You've got to learn your lines better," he said to me. "You've got the whole back of the shul giving you the Amen, but you can't get stuck in that place, in that slow kaddish. Get through that and learn speed."

He is accustomed to learning lines and regards me as a slow study.

On Shabbos services Fran hears him bawl me out.

She says, "Even if you take all day, up there they have to wait."

The actor looks at me impatiently. Still I'm standing in the back row saying my Mourners' Prayer.

This man thinks he's become a giant already.

The PEN Women's Committee is putting on a program, "Ties That Bind: Literary Relationships Among Women." It is our first major presentation as a new committee. Our organizers are Grace Paley and Meredith Tax, but I am cochairing this event with Mary Gordon. I have to get the names of the speakers into the PEN office before departure.

In two days I leave for Israel for the First International Women Writers' Conference, although I never reached the famous Abby Rockefeller. Nor have I yet completed the concept of a closing ritual.

I will travel to Jerusalem with Mary Gordon, room with her and Grace Paley and Marilyn French, and return with Grace Paley. What could be bad about such a conference?

And tonight, in my loft, there is to be a reading from the memoir of my parents, Paul and Beatrice Masserman.

Naomi Newman from San Francisco and Arthur Strimling of the Ballad Theater of New York will be Beatrice and Paul.

While Naomi is here we have had long talks. She makes nesting space in Bob's drawing room: earphones, tapes, pretty spread, incense to encapsulate herself. Now she is preparing for the evening of drama at the loft.

She goes into my linen cabinet for spreads and tablecloths. The guests enter to a loft filled with food and flowers.

We have a beautiful Shabbat, the candle lighting sung in Naomi's sweet voice. Then Ilene Posnick serves challah to the gathered. She describes the making and baking of challah, with honey and love and singing so the bread will braid itself in the rising.

The Leibers, Judith and Gerson, longtime friends, he a painter-printmaker, Judith, a designer of elegant purses, are entranced and somewhat startled by the Hasidic spirit of the group, by our claiming of holiday. Some of my friends look askance, but through poetry and singing the evening unfolds.

Mark Kaminsky reads from *The Book of Esther, Bobbeh Meisehs*, about his grandmother Esther. Kaminsky's poetry/prose is stunning, in the voice of the old woman. He, the disciple of Barbara Myerhoff, has learned the art of tale telling from her.

Tears abound. Mark weeps during the reading of his poem "Naming," calling out the names of his ancestors who have died—children from diseases, aunts from Hitler.

Then Ilene, that sweet bird, sings a Yiddish song dear to her late father, and she breaks down.

Michele Landsberg, my journalist friend from Canada, hides in a corner to smoke and to weep, mourning her mother's recent death.

I rise to introduce Arthur and Naomi as Paul and Bea, the writers of the memoir. As they read, Nahama, my youngest daughter, sits next to me and weeps for her grandfather and her lonely grandmother.

Ultimately, I felt heart's ease, because I had my father's voice returned to me and I had created a way for my parents to speak to each other again.

When it ended, Mark and a dance therapist from Boston began a *klezmer*, Jewish wedding dance, joy after tears.

Mark is an ecstatic, always excited. He rejects those who try to calm him.

"Did they say to Einstein, 'Calm down'?" he asks.

Josh Mailman, a young philanthropist, was so moved he went into Bob's studio alone, regretting that he hadn't brought his elderly father for the evening.

The Leibers sat listening with hidden expressions. I wondered if they were bored. No, they were surreptitiously wiping tears from their eyes. Judith Leiber went into my bedroom and left her "Judith Leiber" purse on my pillow, a snakeskin purse with golden clasps and tiger eyes. Her bags are locked in the jewelry cases of the finest department stores. I had a treasure on my pillow.

When they left, Gus held my hand. I expected him to say something ironic, sarcastic, or dismissive, for he regards me as a sentimental feminist.

He looked at me for a long moment and said, "Take very good care of yourself."

I am finding many ways to honor my parents.

New York, Saturday, March 28

Naomi departs.

This Sabbath, the synagogue did something so humane. They gave a *kiddish* to honor the survivor of the camp, the disturbed gentleman whose present is always the past, who explains to everyone that he is a *gute mensch*, that his papers are okay, that they know him in the old synagogue. He cries out about the shootings he's witnessed in the church, in the field, in the camps.

He talks loudly during service and people try to hush him and once someone even threatened him, and now they honored him.

He wore a nice blue suit with his tallis and yarmulke, and I almost didn't recognize him. He was given an *aliyah*, a turn at the *bima*.

The gentleman came down from the *bima* proudly and shook everyone's hand. When the rabbi, during his sermons, said that they were honoring this man so he would know they were his family, the survivor began shouting and talking again.

"Later, later, we'll talk," said the rabbi, "during the *kiddish*."

The honoree continued shouting.

"Give him medicine," yelled someone.

"Throw him out," suggested another.

Honoring is complicated.

I also found out that the little *kiddish* I'm planning tomorrow is more expensive than I had expected: the custodian has to be given money, sacramental wine has to be served for the blessing. Fran, my blond widow friend, is coming early to help.

The actor preparing for his re–bar mitzvah makes the circular hand signal to speed up as I am saying my kaddish.

Is he the director and I in his production?

I am cranky and perhaps jealous. He is new and honored; I, already established, am, if not attacked, ignored.

Announcements are made at the end of the service. My minyan tomorrow is not mentioned, nor is my pending trip to Jerusalem. The rabbi does not want his congregation to know something subversive is happening.

As I brood when we leave, Bob takes my arm.

"What did *you* hope to get out of the shul?" I ask him.

"My wife," he says. "I can get my wife out of shul, but can I get shul out of my wife?"

New York, Sunday, March 29

A great day.

Outside the synagogue, in a case facing the main street, is the announcement: "Sunday, March 29. After morning services, kiddish with lox."

We begin jamming in. The men trickle in slowly, not even a minyan by 9 A.M., but my women have risen early, dismissed patients, put aside brush and palette, turned off the computer, schlepped down from the upper West Side, the upper East Side, and from Brooklyn. Beautiful they are, and I am proud. They enter respectfully and seriously and with great presence.

They spill over onto the rows reserved for men and the *mekhitza* can't cover them and the men have to sit within close range of women and we have to daven together in serious pursuit.

Our reader today is a sweet singer, a burly man with a high tenor. He has never looked upon me on a Sunday when he drops in. But there are so many of us today, thirteen, that he has to take note.

Seven of us are the Seder Sisters, part of a group of women that has celebrated a feminist Passover together since 1976. Every year since then we have read *The Women's Haggadah,* which I coauthored with Naomi Nimrod in Israel back in 1975. That is our text, made sacred by the inclusion of our foremothers.

Among the Sisters are Letty Cottin Pogrebin, formally dressed, her hair in a bun, and Michele Landsberg, who, although totally disapproving of separate seating, rushed down with a taxi from the Canadian consulate.

"I understand the need to mourn for one's parents," she says.

And we are also rich in psychiatrists, analysts, and psychologists, including my psychologist daughter Nahama. In case our presence causes more than distraction, these women are trained to soothe the wild beast.

Bella Abzug phoned in her regrets. She had to go out of town.

"Remember," she said, "that I said kaddish for my father all those years ago. My grandfather had taught me Hebrew."

She was only thirteen and a girl, rising up every day for the prayer in her Orthodox synagogue. What did she learn from that experience?

"I learned that I can do what I have to do and no one can stop me," said Bella. "But next time you call for a minyan, let me know."

First I move the charity box, the *pushke*, so there will be room for us.

The men stare.

One says, "There must be a minyan of them."

Another, "Do you think they'll want to lead the service next?"

A sourpuss, always giving me dour looks—and he no treat to look at himself—complains, "There'll be more of them than of us."

The sweet blond women in Hadassah, Fran and Sarah, arrive to help me serve the *kiddish*. Look who's coming to set the table, to bring her own egg salad—Doris, my benchmate on that first day!

Every man of that group who had felt impunity in opposing my presence silences or absents himself on this day or sits stiffly and uncomfortably.

My friend Fred sits protectively in a folding chair beside me, next to the women's bench, calling out the pages.

"You're in the wrong pew," says the sourpuss.

Arnold, the sports-reading lawyer, looks around at us.

"All the bases loaded," he says.

After, the rabbi invites everyone for a *kiddish* in honor of my father's memory. Is this what men feel— gratitude and honor and part of a respected lineage?

The rabbi is especially excited this morning, first to have a full house and then to have a full spread.

"If only Tsibble were around," says the rabbi. "How he would enjoy himself!"

"Where is he?" asks Fred, passing around the food.

"I don't know," says the rabbi. "He hasn't been around lately. I don't have an address or phone for him."

"Where does he work?" asks Fred.

"He doesn't work," says the rabbi. "He would carry a lunch box and pretend to go to the garment district, but he hasn't worked in a long time. I gave him fare and a little extra to make up the minyan."

The rabbi cannot refrain from addressing the women.

"Ladies," he says, "I know you're all well thought of in your fields. I hope you will stay close to Judaism and do the work of Torah."

My friends blink. This may not be first on their agenda, but they are friendly to the minyan-goers.

"Remember the old days?" says one elder. "When there was herring, lox, and bagels. And the women were serving us. Remember how nice it was? Where have the women been all these years?"

"Rabbi," I ask, "can we get used to strong women?"

"Sure, sure," he says.

The men reluctantly depart. The shammes leaves smiling, carrying a little bag of leftovers, including a jar of herring, one of the four reasons to live.

My friends and I part.

I am gathering up *kvitels*, written notes, to take to the Western Wall. Doris, the old profane woman, hands me a note calling down curses, she tells me, upon those who have betrayed her. I don't open the tightly folded note, but I'm sure the terrorist trio and Ornstein are more than mentioned.

My Chabad grocer wanted to send a note.

"Write your message and I'll pick it up," I told him.

I went by his grocery two days in a row, and the grocer, gruff and often shouting, had not written the note to put into the Western Wall for God's eyes (and those of the Israeli cleaning machines that clear the crevices periodically and keep all the notes piled in a cave).

I pay one last visit to the grocery before I return home to prepare for departure. The grocer rushes out of the grocery. He didn't trust himself, that patriarch, that master of his family. Instead, his wife wrote the note for God's eyes.

At last I pack.

ℵ

Israel Women's Network, International Conference of Women Writers, Jerusalem, March 29–April 8

We gather, sixty-six women writers from twenty-six countries.

We meet on Rosh Hodesh, the New Moon, to hear welcoming speeches from Teddy Kolleck, the mayor, Shimon Peres, foreign minister, and Alice Shalvi, head of the Israel Women's Network.

Alice makes a speech of mythic reference, surprising for one of Orthodox observance.

She says:

For women in all cultures, in all societies, the moon has traditionally been a very special emblem. Our lives between puberty and menopause, so long as we are fertile, are governed by a monthly cycle. As Diana, goddess of virginity, as Hecate, goddess of witchcraft, and as Lucina, goddess of childbirth, the moon has prefigured varied, contradictory, yet ultimately synthesized aspects of womanhood. . . . The moon is us, ourselves. . . .

Why women writers? Because, increasingly, it is becoming clear to us ourselves that we have a distinctive voice, that women's writing is different in subject matter and theme, in form and in style, that it expresses precisely that flow and flux of which the moon is a symbol. . . .

We accept our difference gratefully, only demanding that it not be made an excuse for discrimination or inequality.

We are meeting primarily to speak to each other, to listen to each other. . . . We are meeting in order to commune in friendship.

During this week, Marilyn French asks and answers, "Is there a women's writing?" She says:

There are in general rough differences in the way males and females approach writing. In general . . . men are interested in the subject of males bolstering their egos; men tend to create characters who live at a distance from their bodies and/or emotions and almost always from other people; and they tend to be concerned with . . . competition, rivalry, and violence.

Women tend to create characters who are connected to their feelings and sometimes even to their bodies, and usually to other people. They tend to find loneliness . . . tragic. . . . And they are concerned with . . . harmony, giving nourishment to others, and cooperation.

She bases her remarks upon scholarly analyses of short stories and mysteries by both genders. She is rigorously opposed by the imposing figure of Shulamith HaRaven, Israeli novelist, who takes the position that writing has no gender and who refuses to be known as a woman writer.

We gather for six days, living in the artists' quarters belonging to the city, on a promontory with a view of the wall around the Old City.

We listen to each other reading, to the works of Margaret Drabble and Eve Figues from Great Britain, of Buchi Emecheta from Great Britain and Nigeria, of Flora Nwapa of Nigeria. We listen to Gerd Brantenberg of Norway, to the beautiful poetry of Vilborg Dagjarsdottir of Iceland, to the speech by Sana Hassan, originally of Egypt, to a play of Sandra Shotlander of Australia, to the poetic memoir of Joy Kagawa of Canada, to those of us from the States: the poets Alicia Ostriker and Irena Kelpfisz, and fiction writers Marilyn French, Grace Paley, Mary Gordon, Rosellen Brown, and myself. We hear Israeli poets like Shirley Kaufman.

And we tour and we play.

On one tour into the Negev, the bus stops at the Dead Sea (*Yam Ha Melach*, the Salt Sea). The women float on the heavy waters, where it is difficult to sink. Marilyn French leads the women in a Busby Berkeley water ballet, singing, "A Pretty Girl Is like a Melody," kick, kick. From the shore a husky-voiced man joins in.

Mostly, sharing rooms, suites together, gathering at night at restaurants, staying up late to watch the sun rise over the stone walls of the Old City, we learn about one another.

In the end, I deal with the closing ceremony.

First we rewrite the traditional words of the psalmist, "Here life is sweet and pleasant. Let us sit, brothers, together." Only we sit with our sisters, exchanging *achim*, brothers, for *nashim*, women.

I ask the women, seated before us on the floor, to come forward and translate the song into their tongue. They rise and form a line. We hear the psalmist's words in Chinese, Nepalese, Japanese, Filipino, Ibo, Polish, Russian, Serbo-Croatian, Hungarian, Finnish, Norwegian, German, Danish, Dutch, Spanish, Flemish, French (*"ici si bon et si plaisant / assions ensemble mes soeurs"*), Icelandic, and "outback Aussie," besides the Hebrew of our hosts and English of the United Kingdom, Canada, and the U.S.

We are of many languages, but of one heart.

I have been reading a prayer every morning for months. I revise it.

First I ask a Scottish Jew, Linda Robinson, to blow the shofar, the ram's horn, which is sounded at the time of the New Moon, holidays, and impending war. I ask that it be sounded for our gathering:

> Sound the Ram's Horn
> For our freedom
> Raise the banners
> To gather us
> From the four corners of the earth,
> Women who have been in exile
> From one another,
> Dispersed throughout the nations,
> Are *now* a nation.

Alice Shalvi translates the morning prayer into Hebrew.

I then say:

> We are about to make a curious card together, a magical card, a card of relics for the Israel Women's

Network, bits of ourselves, a thatching, a patching of power.

Will you each clip a lock, a bit of hair, and tape it down, glue it down to the card, with your name next to the lock? This will be called a hair card, much more powerful than a hair shirt.

In times of trouble, the Israel Women's Network can take the card and call upon it.

Then all of us, we hairy creatures, from the four corners of the earth, will send forth our power.

The hair card is a palette of color: gray, blond, salt and pepper, red, black.

We sing and beat upon our tambourines and dance the hora, all of us—those native to our lands, those in exile (Louisa Valenzuela in exile from Argentina), those honored, those obscure. But our curls of hair rest cozily on the card.

I ask us to take the famous Jerusalem oath: "If I forget thee, O Jerusalem Conference of Women Writers, may my pen lose its point!"

I stay an extra couple of days and fly back with Grace Paley.

New York, Wednesday, April 8

"The lady's back!" says Rodney, lisping.

Larry, the button man, seems to have aged even during my brief absence. Fred is wearing a warm vest to protect his chest. He has been down with the flu more than once this winter.

I would feel loved if Joshua, that curious person, hadn't pushed the curtain in front of me.

"I saw you on TV last night," he says.

It was on a holiday documentary in which I was a participant.

"That's right," I say.

He sees his group watching.

"Blasphemer!" he calls me.

Dad, I say, news item. While I was gone the Baby M case was settled. The baby was awarded to the sperm donor, William Stern. Mary Beth Whitehead, the birth mother, was stripped of all privileges.

Judge Harvey Sorkow's decision legitimates surrogate contracts.

In his judgment, he characterized the mother as "manipulative, impulsive, and exploitive" in her insistence on keeping the baby.

Mary Beth Whitehead will appeal.

My father would ask, What does this have to do with the Jews?

The judge and the donor, Dad.

⧆

New York, Tuesday, April 14

Okay, Dad, I say, here's the date, and what happened?

I tell him. Gorbachev of the U.S.S.R. proposes a missile-free Europe. The American Secretary of State Schultz in Moscow rejects the offer.

We've got to sell our missiles someplace, my dad would have said archly.

LEISURE WORLD

I'm not there, but I walk along the paths that Dad took to Club House Four, although he often lost his way going or coming.

A fellow club member once bawled him out.

"How can you keep walking the same path and not know where you're agoing?"

My father said, "I always drove. I never walked."

Dad told me, "They emasculated me when they took away my driver's license."

But even in Detroit, young and middle aged, he was not a good driver. He was always being stopped and ticketed. Dad would be thinking of domestic or foreign policy as he drove right through red lights and stop signs.

Yet he always knew where he was going, the moral path, the caring way.

The club member who criticized Dad for his lack of sense of direction also bawled him out in the club house pool, saying, "You tread water. You only stay in the shallow end."

My dad smiled at him and did not reply.

The club member thought my father was a softy.

But Dad knew when to swim into the deep.

New York, Wednesday, April 15

Tonight was our Twelfth Annual Women's Seder.

What would the rabbi say to my coauthored *The Women's Haggadah* with its paean to biblical women? What would he say to our regendering the traditional holiday of Passover and making it our own?

He would likely say, "No men? What kind of holiday without men?"

We gathered, seated on pillows on the floor, mothers and daughters and even a granddaughter.

Our theme is loss—my obsession this year. And others, members of this seder community, speak of loss of a husband, family separated, family divorced, mothers gone.

We name ourselves by our matrilineage. We tell our tales, lament our plagues, sing our gatherings.

We bless one another and are blessed in turn.

I have been on the moon. Or I will feel so when I return to the synagogue tomorrow.

New York, Sunday, April 19

I have dinner with the stockbroker. He reads the rewritten first act carefully. He flicks his cigar. Ashes fall on the page.

"Who should I call about this play?" he asks, tapping the cover of the manuscript, which I had bound for him. "Joe Papp at the Public or Davidson at Mark Taper in L.A.?"

I begin to levitate from the table.

"But it needs work," he says, signaling for the check. "It's not theatrical yet."

I fall back into my seat.

New York, Wednesday, April 22

Joshua comes into shul, kisses the mezuzah, then proceeds to step on my feet in order to pull the *mekhitza* across my face.

This happened earlier in the week, not with Joshua but with an intense, dark-bearded young man who came from nowhere and entered our little prayer room and whose first action was to pull the curtain.

"Only the rabbi touches the curtain," I said. "Only he adjusts it, not every passerby."

"Then I can't pray," he said and rushed out of the synagogue.

This young man, since, has davened in the corridor in order to be away from me, even when the curtain was partially pulled. I recognize this fellow as a *baal tshuv*, a prodigal son, one who wandered and returned. But this wanderer is on the path to fanaticism. It's as if he has no shape without being ruled, without adherence to dicta. I have seen these boys also in Israel, from the States, their beards new grown, the ideas newly hatched, and, with it all, intolerance.

I now realize that six of Rabbi Ornstein's followers will threaten the minyan by refusing to attend if there is not adherence to their way.

So, this morning, about ten minutes to eight, Joshua is blithely pulling the curtain and I repeat what I had said to the intense young man, "Only the rabbi touches the curtain."

Schlomo enters the fray. He begins to shout.

"You have no right to tell us what to do. According to Jewish law, you don't even have a soul. I am a responsible member of the congregation. You aren't even a person according to the shul. You aren't a member. You can't vote. And you are breaking the law."

I think of my father and his presuffrage high school teacher who could vote only by proxy, through another, by advising the janitor.

Schlomo keeps shouting and interrupting the davening.

"Your father is being insulted. My father is turning over in his grave."

"You don't have a father," I say. "You were stamped out in a matzo mill."

The davener is Ralph, the caring fellow in his late thirties, who attends seriously to the business at hand, like preventing Fred from smoking or joking during services. As the ranting and raving continue, Ralph stops davening. He never turns toward me, but I can see from the stiffness of his neck, the twitching of his back, that he is angry.

"Don't touch the *mekhitza*," I whisper fiercely to Joshua. "Shut up!" I say to Schlomo.

Schlomo goes into the corridor to shout more of the same.

"She is not a person. She is not even a member of the congregation and, therefore, has no rights."

The pages of the siddur blur before me.

Our sexton, my dear mentor and scold, has had pneumonia, and his substitute is Rodney, the man of ninety-seven, who enjoys the prestige of substitute shammes. He goes into the corridor to speak to the ranter and comes shuffling back in.

"Young lady," he says through his gums, "why are you making such a fuss? It's a little thing, that curtain. Why are you holding up services?"

At the end of the service, Ralph says, "Tomorrow you bring the scissors and I'll cut down the *mekhitza*."

The rabbi has entered.

"Come into my office," he says, "to make peace."

The men follow me in.

The rabbi says, "I can do with or without a *mekhitza*, but the more religious members of the shul, the ones who daven here daily, want one."

I say, "Rabbi, then I will be the daily object of insult. I will always be in the position of needing to be protected."

The rabbi says, "So, I'll protect you."

"Then," I say, "the whole shul is rotten to the foundation if it listens to a small, fanatical group in order to isolate women from the service."

The Fanatical Trio and Ornstein heckle.

They have the rabbi on their side.

I go to my office in the Writers' Room. I have been writing and rewriting laments for the silent mothers of the Jewish Bible, the Christian Testament, and the Koran. This is the song of the mother, Sarah.

SARAH'S LAMENT

I did not think when that other,
the small dark one, went with his mother
and a skin of water into the desert,
that it would happen to me.
But Isaac has been taken, hurriedly.
I ask, "Where is he, my son, my only one,
who filled my ancient breasts with milk
and my mouth with laughter?"

The servants run away and hide.
I ask the woman tending the herd,
"Have you seen him, my son,
my only one?" She averts her face.
I ask at the walls, the oases,
the places of palm and date,
"Where is he gone, my son, my only one?"
They look up at the clear sky and shake their
heads.

And the wind has blown across their steps.
The sand has filled in their footfall.
If I look up at the sun, my eyes burn.

I will never see clearly again.
There is nothing for me to see again.
There has been a secret kept from me.
A father secret. A father-right,
so brutal, so cruel
that if he were to come to my tent,
I would turn my back upon him.

To take what is born in laughter,
to hear his last shriek of terror.
Dark against the sun they come.
They do not walk together,
the son and the father.
He comes to my tent, my son, my only one.
He sleeps in my tent.
He will bring his bride to my tent.
We have no need of him
who calls himself the man of God.
We have no need of the one
who fetters his child.

As for Isaac, my almost-lost,
all of his days the knife will glisten in the
sun.
He will grow into a whiny, foolish old man,
and become his own father.

New York, Thursday, April 23

The rabbi comes in half an hour early to make sure
no one will insult me. The intense young man is back,
brought in from the corridor to make up a minyan. The
mekhitza is partially pulled. The young man is some-

what satisfied. But the serious fellow, Ralph, who was to cut down the *mekhitza,* has not shown up.

I have been up all night wondering what to do. I was having a Talmudic argument with myself. If I brought the scissors and he cut the curtain down, whose action was it? Wasn't I mature enough to complete the action myself instead of relying upon him? What if we cut down the *mekhitza?* Will this mean bringing down the wrath of the rabbi and that I will be barred from services?

And, then, what about my saying kaddish and honoring my father?

I never slept last night.

I stuck the sharp small scissors, last used on the shower curtains, into my change purse and left for the synagogue especially early. But Ralph was not there.

Okay, I think, then it's up to me, and that shouldn't be a surprise. Can I get up the nerve to cut down the *mekhitza?*

Just then, also early, the rabbi shows up to protect me. I go home with the scissors. I put them away. What's the use?

New York, Friday, April 24

Today I come in a bit early. The *mekhitza* is lying crumpled on the floor, the strings hanging from the ceiling. There it is—this object of my rage and wrath and humiliation, this insistence by a small group of men on power by separation—lying in a corner, the rod broken, slashed, useless, with Ralph's card lying on top of it.

The old substitute sexton, Rodney, shuffles in.

"Is this your work?" Rodney frowns at me.

"No!" I say, stunned.

"I did it," says Ralph. "I cut the strings, I broke the rod, I slashed the curtains and put them over there in the corner, and I left my calling card on top."

Larry comes in and raises his eyebrow.

"I did it," says Ralph. "I cut the strings, I broke the rod, I slashed the curtains and put them over there in the corner. If you don't believe me, my calling card is on top."

Arnold arrives with the sports section. He stops.

"Foul play," he says.

Ralph accepts responsibility over and over during the morning's services. To my astonishment, the other men, even my grocer, say nothing.

Yesterday, when there was reading from the Torah, my grocer was asked to carry the Torah around the room. He avoided my bench where I and another woman, she waiting to give the rabbi the name of her new granddaughter for a blessing, stood ready to kiss the blue velvet casing.

"Aw, c'mon," said Fred. "Give the ladies a break."

Next time around the grocer, staring straight ahead, paused in front of me.

Today the grocer is surprised to see no *mekhitza*. He is uncomfortable but does not get up to leave in rage. It's unclear to me why he stays or why, when he is rushing out to tend his store, he pauses for a moment respectfully during my saying of the final kaddish.

He greets me at each shopping trip to his grocery with, "How are you, Doctor?"

He is ardent in his belief but not punitive.

So here is a roomful of men, davening, not commenting, and the *mekhitza* is down and the strings are hanging in the air.

Ralph has put on his tam and is on his way to work nearby. I give up swimming at the Y to catch up with him.

"I couldn't come in yesterday," says Ralph. "I was so upset by the attack. I realized he was attacking you only because you were a woman."

I wanted to say, *"Boker Tov, Eliahu,"* Good morning, Elijah, as the Israelis remark upon a belated discovery.

I hold out my hand to shake Ralph's. I don't know if he's too Orthodox to let me touch his hand. Instead, he kisses me.

"You're wonderful," he says, to my astonishment.

Why am I wonderful when he did such an act of conscience?

There was, *takeh,* indeed, a palace revolt today.

New York, Monday, April 27

Dad, I say, you've missed the news.

Who: Major General Richard Secord. Where: the Tower panel.

Major Secord testified that President Reagan knew of the diversion of funds from Iran arms sales to the Contras of Nicaragua.

Surprise! my Dad would say.

The rabbi is still worried that there won't be enough for a minyan. I wonder if he is thinking of canceling our particular minyan altogether.

If so, do I rise at 5 A.M. and go through the battle all over with another—or the same—group?

I phone Alice Shalvi in Jerusalem to wish her *Shabbat Shalom,* a Sabbath of peace, and to hear how she recovered from the Women Writers' Conference. I also tell her about the palace revolt.

"Write a play," says Alice laughing. "There's your revenge."

"I am, Alice," I say.

She pauses. She was only kidding. I wonder how all this sits with her, she who accepts the tenets of Orthodoxy, who worships behind a *mekhitza*.

Cigar phones from his stockbrokerage.

"I only have a minute," he says, "but I've been thinking about our play."

(Our?)

"This is what you have to know. What the audience wants is a refuge, a safe place. That's the *raison* of theater. You have to provide a sanctuary. This is too angry. Try again."

A sanctuary, with all the *meshugoyim*, the madmen, that lie in wait for me?

∾

New York, Tuesday, April 23

I am writing "Hagar's Lament": Hagar speaks of Sarah, with whom she shares the tent. Perhaps *I* am Hagar, the outcast.

> In the tent she cast an evil eye upon me
> and the child dropped from me.
> The angels tell me he will be bound to God
> But that mark upon him by the knife of his
> father,
> That name given him by his father,

what availed us that,
the Egyptian and her son?

But we lived.
He learned the ways of the arrow.
I found him his bride out of Egypt.
But when I saw his father,
an old man, walking his other son to Moriah,
the boy carrying the faggots of sacrifice,
how I laughed!
For there she must be in her tent,
she the witch,
she, tearing her hair, cursing, pleading,
but we, she and I,
are the same to him,
mothers of sons to be sacrificed.

The more I reread the same prayers, the more I begin to question.

I begin to think also of Mary, of the completed sacrifice:

He lay on my lap,
stiffening, heavy.
You say he is risen.
Why is my lap still dented?

Is anything worth the sacrifice of one's children? I will never believe it.

New York, Wednesday, April 29

Our sexton is out with pneumonia.
There is something missing in the morning service, a crankiness, orderliness, and enthusiasm.

Yesterday the shul was a zoo. The tenth man was an obese, gray-haired guy, somewhat retarded, who never opened a prayer book but spent the entire service digging into his pockets for hard candies and sucking them noisily.

There is a new member, an international lawyer named Charles, from Paris. He is Orthodox, covering his face with his fine linen tallis before he dons the tallis, standing throughout the service. Yet my presence and the absence of a *mekhitza* do not seem to faze him. There is something Gallic in this, a level of tolerance. Or is it that if the woman is personable, one's objections are moderated?

In the midst of the service a gray-haired woman enters in stocking feet. I look at her white socks and think that she is being respectful, like taking off shoes before entering a mosque. She goes to the end of my bench, lifts up my pretty purple jacket, and places it over her head. I quietly remove it from her and fold it back on the bench. She is annoyed with me and moves to the men's side. They start to get excited, which only excites her the more. Also, she is smoking. It is forbidden to smoke during services.

"Put out your cigarette!" they yell.

She sees the prayer books in their boxes, and she lifts them out and hurls them into the air, yelling "Hell! Shit! Damn!" with each book.

The men become acrobats, trying to catch the prayer books before they hit the ground. She grabs for my coat again. The whole room is in an uproar except for the tenth man, who is unwrapping his sugar candy. The men yell, she becomes more excited, and I usher her out.

I realize that she is the quintessence of woman to them, of their fear of what I would do if not contained

at least by a curtain. I would be wild, desecrate the place, speak with foul tongue, be profane. And they do all in their might to keep this from happening.

"Who is she?" I ask the rabbi.

"A well-known drunk," he says. "A mental case."

It amuses me to think that on this street where every other doorway is occupied by some destitute or drunken person, she has made the "well-known" category.

After services, Fred goes to get coffee and gets me, for treats, a corn muffin. The tenth man is also there, eyeing the muffin.

"Aw, give me a bite, just a tiny bite, just a morsel," he begs.

Fred asks would I mind if he breaks off a piece for the guy.

"It's the best muffin I've ever tasted," the fellow says, smacking his lips. "What's the recipe? Where did you get it?"

Every luncheon counter, every deli in New York sells these corn muffins.

Fred tells another Ten Commandments joke.

God is thinking about to whom he should offer his commandments. He tries the Tartars. "Thou shalt not kill" is the first commandment.

"You gotta be crazy," says the Tartar.

So God approaches a Babylonian.

"Give me an example," says the Babylonian.

"Thou shalt not steal."

"Forget it," says the Babylonian.

So God approaches the Jews. There, in Egypt, he finds Moses. "How would you like to follow my commandments?" God asks.

"First of all," says Moses, "how much do they cost?"

"They're free," says God.

"I'll take ten," Moses says.

Today I see the tenth man at my local coffee shop, taking up two seats at the counter, buttering his corn muffin, licking the grease off his fingers.

One of our athletic members tells me, "I knew you were swimming the other day."

"How did you know?"

"I saw your yarmulke outside the women's locker room."

New York, Thursday, May 7

Bob is finishing up the semester at The Cooper Union, a school in Greenwich Village founded a hundred years ago by Peter Cooper that subsidizes the gifted students of art, engineering, and architecture. He has held final critiques in etching and in experimental printmaking, and his last day of class is tomorrow. The whole school then gets ready for the big studio show that takes over the entire building.

The big news is that on May 11 the rabbi has called for a vote on women becoming full voting members of *Beit Hatikva*.

"It's stacked," Fred reassured me. "He'll call out his cronies."

But I worry. It was just voted down a couple of months ago. I had inquired at other Orthodox synagogues to see if they had women as members. The Charles Street Synagogue has full membership, as does Lincoln Square, which my rabbi regards as the frontrunner in modern Orthodoxy.

Last Sunday, my friend Alice Shalvi flew in from Israel to become the first woman to speak from the *bima*, the pulpit, of Lincoln Square Synagogue.

She said, in her usual modest way, "It went very well."

That weekend also she had been brought in by the Woodmere Synagogue of Long Island. That Conservative synagogue has been moving toward Orthodoxy, removing women from visibility. Hearing that Alice was scheduled as a speaker, the more fundamentalist members of the group threatened to stage a walkout.

"Instead," said Alice, "more people attended than at any time since Yom Kippur."

She has raised forty-two thousand dollars for her modern Orthodox girls' high school based on scholarship and participatory democracy, so her trip, though exhausting, has not been a waste.

She needs this courage to bring home. Her school is often under attack by Jewish fundamentalists.

She sighs. "I did not know when I walked a less-trodden path what I would encounter. I met with anger, with opposition. I want to be accepted. And yet I do not go the common route."

Last night we sat in a cafe in Lincoln Center having a half-carafe of wine and a salad and giggling and then bursting into tears, for our lives are worthy of both expressions.

"This morning," said Alice, "I rose full of vigor, walked from Seventieth Street to One Hundredth, walked through the park, and everywhere were tractors turning the earth, were workmen beautifying the park, were mothers and children. The city has declared an end to winter."

Yesterday we had our windows washed, so winter has officially ended with its detritus removed.

New York, Friday, May 8

Obit, Dad. Rita Hayworth died at the age of sixty-eight of Alzheimer's disease.

Ah, he would have said, the Love Goddess, the poor thing.

I am in terror writing my ten-minute speech for PEN, my first public appearance before my professional organization. My speech is not exactly to the point of the program, "Literary Relationships Among Women." My remarks are about historical figures in the Labor Archives and their effect upon me.

I will begin my remarks:

> I will speak of three writers: one, Mary Heaton Vorse, a well-known journalist in her time and much published; the next, Matilda Robbins, whose work is largely in archives but whose articles were published in IWW magazines; and the third, an anonymous woman, and all I know of her is her short autobiographical statement on her application form to Brookwood Labor School.

I worry how to make my statement something beyond the personal. I worry how to persuade the listener about the excitement of the archives, of their influence upon one's fiction, and of the discovery of historical figures who become one's mentors and lead into knowledge of the past.

The PEN Women's Committee insisted upon itself, insisted upon being formed to make up for the lack of recognition of women in the largest writers' organization. This lack came to the fore at the international PEN meeting, where few women appeared on panels or were under discussion or gave readings. It was a much-ballyhooed event, with daily coverage in the *New York Times*, but we were invisible. This is our first large event, and we are anxious lest we fail.

New York, Saturday, May 9

Kaddish and more kaddish. I say it four times a morning. I still stumble over the long first kaddish, *Kaddish de Rabbanan*, for the teachers and teachers of teachers and all their disciples, to all who study Torah, let there be peace and loving-kindness and let us say, Amen.

May is the time of multiple celebration in our family. Three of our four children were born during this month. I always feel pregnant during May and buy lilacs in season, for I carried a branch of lilacs with me into the labor room. My twin sons were born on Mother's Day.

I remember how Bob and I each carried a baby wrapped in a receiving blanket out of Sinai Hospital in New York. A white-jacketed doctor held the outer door open for us and said, "How ingenious of you."

I have been informed that I am to be rehired at the college in Westchester. The college is renowned for its departments of the arts: theater, art, writing, music. The majority of the faculty is adjunct. Thus money is saved on health plans, pensions, sabbaticals. And yet all the artists, the writers, actors, musicians, and painters of New York fight to teach there.

We have been commuting for five years from Detroit to New York, but with this year's grant, I have stopped commuting to the Midwest.

How can one be in two cities teaching writing and still write?

℞

New York, Sunday, May 10

This morning, the makings for the next *mekhitza*. Is it the sixth? It is a beige, cheap curtain thing, lying unassembled in the rabbi's office. I had come with a contribution and thought about withholding the check, but the shul has been there for me—to the extent that I have had a place to honor my father.

As long as the curtain was down Bob was getting up early and rushing over to help make up the minyan. He won't join the service when we're separated by a curtain.

Arnold is missing. I learn the story from Fred.

There was a membership meeting last night. Women's votes didn't come up. But another matter did. Should the synagogue provide meeting space for Alcoholics Anonymous? Several of the members are vociferously against it.

"They could fall and hurt themselves and sue us," says Joshua.

That's when Arnold stands up.

"If you're talking about the law, then it's time for me to speak. I am a former alcoholic. I lost my wife, visiting rights with my child, my job, and I was disbarred.

You see me now. I am a working lawyer. I also help out at the synagogue. This is what a reformed alcoholic looks like."

He sits down quietly. AA will meet at the shul.

Arnold is a hero, bigger than Babe Ruth or Hank Greenberg.

Leisure World, Early January

Bob and my father trade stories about the Hearst newspaper, the *Detroit Times*, for which they both worked, Bob in the art department and as art critic, and my father as everything from rewrite to outstate to head writer to makeup to being on the Teletype.

"Remember Red Monahan?" Dad asks Bob.

We all know the story, but a good story should be told again and again.

"We had two chapters of the AA on copy desk alone," said my Dad, "not to mention the chapter for the photographers.

"One day Red Monohan went to the barber. He'd bent the elbow with preholiday cheer.

" 'Cut my hair,' Red said to the barber.

" 'Where?' asked the barber.

"Red Monahan, whose name describes his hair, rubbed his hand vaguely over his head.

" 'Here,' he said and quickly fell asleep in the barber chair. When he awoke, his head had been shaved!

"He was on rewrite, getting the stories over the phone and rewriting them. He never took off his hat. He squashed the earphones down over it.

"We used to send our stories down the chute to the printers with a note attached, 'Head to follow.' One day Red sent down his hat, with the note pinned to the hat, 'Head to follow.'"

"Remember Hymie, the photographer?" asks Bob.

"Who wouldn't?" says my father.

"One day Hymie had a bit of a nip and saw someone unwrapping their lunch sandwich. 'Give me a taste,' he begged. The other photographer refused. 'If I can't eat it, then you can't,' said Hymie and spit on the sandwich. Then he turned and spit on his own. 'And you can't have this one either.'"

My mother made a face.

"There's another Hymie story," said Bob.

"Hymie found an eagle frozen on an ice floe in the Detroit River. He got a call that an eagle was there, stunned and its feathers stuck together with tar. So Hymie nonchalantly drove out to the river, picked up the bird from the ice, tucked it under his arm like a chicken, and brought it down to the *Times* to photograph.

"I saw him going through the art department with this eagle and I followed him. He propped up the bird and kept knocking so it would sit alertly, set up the lights, and began photographing it as if it were a studio model.

"Under the lights, the bird defrosted. It began turning its head, opened its beak, and stretched out its claws. Hymie called up the Detroit Zoological Gardens. 'Better hurry it right in,' they advised.

"Hymie stuck the eagle in a cardboard box and began running out of the editorial room through the art department. I saw the claws dig right through the box.

"He got some poor guy to drive him, and, after, that fellow said his upholstery was torn to shreds by the time they reached the zoo. At the zoo, Hymie said, they threw the bird a mouse, which he caught and swallowed in one gulp."

"*Meshuganeh* people," said my mother.

"Remember the tallest man in the world?" asks my father. "He came down to be photographed. And the shortest?"

"Remember the buggy left in the lobby," says Bob, "near the elevator in the lobby? I was going down to lunch and there was the buggy. I looked around. No one was there. Then I saw the note: 'Take care of my baby. I have no money and no welfare.'"

"You phoned and asked me if we wanted another baby," I say. "The kids jumped up and down. 'Yes! Yes! Bring it home.'"

"I took him upstairs to the women of the women's page, but they didn't know how to change a baby, so I changed it and we began phoning around. By that time the woman identified herself and we got her on welfare," Bob finishes the story.

My dad says, "There were ups and downs, but those were the days!"

"The death of the *Times* was terrible," says my mother. "They killed the paper in the dark of night."

"The *Detroit News* bought it out and sent all of us telegrams that our jobs were terminated," says Dad. "My telegram was delivered at 2 A.M."

"For years," says my mother, "they had a reunion on that date at the press club, saying kaddish for the *Times*."

New York, May

The re–bar mitzvah actor is around a lot lately. He has been arguing with me.

"We should say a special kaddish for those who died of AIDS," I suggest to the rabbi.

"They're on their own," says the actor.

"When you're dead, you're on your own?" I ask him. "Then how about your father and my father? And why are we in daily attendance here?"

"Don't overact," he says.

The actor often reads from the Torah on the Sabbath. He sits on the high armchair on the *bima*. He came to services long after I and soon ascended to the *bima*, and I still fight to sit in the middle of the last row rather than in the women's ghetto on Saturdays.

"How about the kaddish for AIDS victims?" I ask the rabbi.

"They're on their own," he says.

But the women, he assures me, will not be on their own.

The big vote for women in the shul was only a preliminary step. Eighteen out of twenty of the membership committee voted to include women. Now it has to go to the entire membership (male), where it needs a two-thirds vote.

New York, Tuesday, May 12

The *mekhitza* is lying across the women's bench, entangled in old tallises that the congregants discarded. This curtain is yellowed lace.

I move the whole lot to the back bench of the men's section. First it was lying around the rabbi's office; now it's scrambled in the prayer room.

Arnold puts down his newspaper.

"You've got to know who to blame," he says. "It's the rabbi. What he wants, he gets. Before this, he did not want women to get membership. He cornered all his friends in the kitchen before the meeting, and he defeated it. Whatever happens is what he wants to have happen."

I am shocked.

"The hardest thing," says the counselor, "is to blame the one you love."

I have been sentimental, although now I see that the rabbi has tired, tired of all the effort, of the attention my "case" requires. His smile has been slipping. He was looking distracted when we met.

"The men asked so modestly," said the rabbi, "so quietly for the *mekhitza*. They admitted they would really like it—the grocer, the Professor, the one who will be the new reader. They really want it."

"I really don't want it," I say.

He shrugs. He doesn't have to say it. I'm not a member of the minyan. I'm not a voting member of the synagogue. And more, I'm a pest. During Sabbath services the head of the Sisterhood scowls at my sitting with Bob and not to the extreme side, where she parades that aisle making sure all the women are ushered there. The followers of the rabbi without synagogue now have a synagogue.

I am depressed all the day. I was grave this afternoon, working on the memoir. There was a power failure and I lost my editing.

Then Bob and I walk through Union Square. It is the day for the farmer's market. I choose spring vegetables and flowers and my spirits rise. Customers are walking bushes and plants as they carry their purchases away.

I need the ingredients for spaghetti. It's the year-end story marathon of my writing class. A special van from the Westchester campus drives them in. They are dressed in bright, light, warm-weather attire. We eat the spaghetti and we read the last stories of the semester and they are very good. Then we lean back, laugh, and gossip until the students board the van, out of Manhattan to the leafy campus.

℞

New York, Wednesday, May 13

I sleep late for the first time in a month. I feel better. I remember advice from the psychiatrist Lilly Engler: "Set a finite time to mourn. Take control. Don't be passive."

I will attend House of Hope for Saturday and maybe Sunday services. I won't stand behind the curtain.

All in all, it shocks me to think how much energy, thought, time, even money was spent on the part of the synagogue these past four months to keep one woman in her place.

And, thereby, all women.

P.M.

I meet with Mike Posnick, head of the new theater, Mosaic, at the Y on Ninety-second Street. We have a business lunch.

I then tell Mike my odyssey with the synagogue. He listens unsympathetically. He leans back against the booth in the pub where we are lunching.

"Your mistake is that you went into a fish store," he says, "and asked for chicken."

So I go back to the House of Hope.

164

New York, Thursday, May 14

Whether chicken or fish, it was business as usual at the shul. I'd missed synagogue yesterday on purpose when the rabbi said the curtain was going up. It was still down today, lying across the women's bench.

Only four or five of us showed up for services, besides the president of an Orthodox shul who came for *yahrzeit*, the yearly anniversary of a death. His shul did not provide a kaddish. Without a minyan, neither could we.

Perhaps the rabbi is ashamed that his synagogue, which prides itself on being the kaddish shul, could not provide it this morning. He speaks to his Orthodox friend.

"When I came to this shul, they told me there was no *mekhitza* and if I believed in a *mekhitza* I should not accept the pulpit. I said, 'But what if the members themselves rise and demand a *mekhitza*?' Today, synagogues are becoming more Orthodox. Young men are coming out of the yeshivas with more learning in the tradition. And they are demanding a *mekhitza*." He is talking earnestly.

I am sitting like a fool on the opposite side of the room. It does not matter that I stood near the curtain, kept to the bench, that I was pleasant, friendly, trusted the rabbi, or took the group into my heart. I am the Other, sitting there, not privy to the rabbi's remarks.

With our shammes in the hospital, I am ignored more than ever.

I rise, return the prayer book, take off my yarmulke, and lift up my gym bag with my swimming clothes.

"Do you realize, Rabbi," I say, as he lifts his eyes, surprised to hear me speaking, "that for the last four months all that effort, that energy, that time, even that expense . . . "

He interrupts, smiling. He thinks I am going to compliment him.

"Yes, yes," he says.

I go on, ". . . was spent against one woman."

The actor, the re–bar mitzvah, says, "You don't know the reasons. You don't know anything about it."

"Don't read me your lines," I tell him.

"Now you're yelling at *me!*" he says.

The men are staring at me. I am clearly the hysterical woman, the interrupter, the one in the way of progress or regress. I am the bag lady who came in and profaned the service.

I stamp out.

The shul has lost Ralph, the spiritual, intelligent man who cut down the *mekhitza*.

"I can't stand the arguing, Fred," he tells my friend.

"I'll miss you, Ralph," says Fred.

"And I'll miss you too, Fred."

Ralph packs his tallis bag and is ready to leave.

"Tsibble is gone," he says, "and the laughter is gone from the place."

Arnold looks around and says, "We'll need a pinch hitter."

P.M.

My nights have nothing to do with my days. I am two separate people. Is anyone the same, I begin to wonder, the entire day?

This is the Thursday when our Women's Committee of PEN American Center presents "Ties That Bind: Literary Relationships Among Women."

Will anyone come?

I arrive early to make sure my panelists are there and find the room already packed. As the program commences, people are jamming in, pounding on the door, blocking the hallway, filling the stairs, standing outside 568 Broadway, wondering if they'll gain entrance.

This program changes our status in PEN. We are no longer only the rebellious daughters. We're the crowd catchers.

Mary Gordon gives a witty introduction. Vivian Gornick is learned and lucid on Zona Gale and Margery Latimer. Grace Paley, short story writer, and Jane Cooper, poet, reminisce about their years together at the Westchester college, both teaching and teaching each other.

Alice Childress, the playwright, speaks of how her grandmother raised her and set her an example and enheartened her to write. Her grandmother kept all the scraps of paper on which the child Alice wrote.

The Argentinean writer Louisa Valenzuela speaks of her mother, also a writer, and both the sharing and competition between them.

The program is much too long. The program is uneven.

The evening is glorious.

New York, Friday, May 15

Fred has phoned two days in a row. He thinks of leaving the synagogue. Bob talks to him one night when I'm out.

"I want to get out," Fred says, "but if not for the rabbi, I'd be sitting in my kitchenette now, two years later. He would phone, 'Put on your pants. We need a man.' I never thought I'd get out of my pajamas. So, I went, davened, had *kiddish,* some joking around, and I was well into the day before it got to me. That's how I got through the last two years."

"Don't drop out," Bob tells him.

But I have.

New York, Saturday, May 16

It's like one of those vaudeville shows advertising "Positively her last appearance." Only she appears again and again. That's what this Kaddish Klub is like.

Fred called. "Sweetheart, we're all so sad. The rabbi's so sad. Tomorrow there's going to be such a nice *kiddish.* It's deli this time. Something different for us. You like the lady who's making it. Her son's being called up to the *bima* before his wedding. The mother's had so much trouble. Now she's trying for a little happiness. Won't you come? And if anybody bothers you, I'll sit near you and tell them to take a fast walk."

So I come. Nobody is really worth so many phone calls and consultations. It's arrogant to assume that one can be an endless subject for discussion. Let it end already.

Not so simple.

I go for the Sabbath services. Of course, the head of Sisterhood is outraged that I'm sitting with my husband, complains to the *gabbai,* who complains to the rabbi to make me move.

She's made everyone else move. All of the women are sitting obediently in a train along the far wall. That far group of rows has only two or three seats in each row. The men have 99 percent of the space now.

The rabbi has come to me for sympathy: "It makes me crazy. She gives a *geshrei,* a yell, 'Control that woman!' The *gabbai* says, 'That woman's got to follow orders.' My dear, I'm the only one on your side."

Should I believe this, Dad? It's good that I was trained early in cynicism.

The rabbi carries the Torah past us this Sabbath morning. Bob takes the fringes of his tallis to kiss the Torah. I move back a bit. The rabbi says, "I'm gladder than you can imagine that you're here."

Fred, of slight build, sits near to ward off anyone who would attack me. Schlomo turns around and glares at us. Gray Braid, who sleeps during services, this time keeps awake to turn his head and righteously stare me down. But the Hadassah women come to sit on the other side of me, and Doris—from that first service—is behind me. Gradually, a sprinkling of women joins us back there.

I say my kaddish, the service ends, the famous deli is about to be served downstairs, but I plan to leave.

Not so fast. The rabbi stops me to tell me his tale as the congregants elbow each other down the stairway to get at the delicatessen.

"Believe me," says the rabbi, "all I want is peace. I tell Ornstein, 'Call off your cohorts; you must leave her alone.'

"'She is a *moredet,* a woman who casts off tradition,' Ornstein says.

"I become angry. 'I will stand by the synagogue door. I will dismiss the minyan if you continue to harass her,'" says the rabbi. "'I have *yichus,* Ornstein. My great-grandfather, my grandfather, father, all great Hasidic rabbis. You, Ornstein, you admire my great-grandfather, the chief rabbi of Prmeshlam, and my grandfather, the rabbi of Zicsloiv, and my father of Noldwarno. I call down curses from my great-grandfather, my grandfather, my father if you don't leave this woman alone, if you don't call off your minions. If you don't do that, your whole life will be cursed.'

"I am assured that Ornstein now understands," the rabbi concludes.

"Darling," says Fred, who is standing behind the rabbi, "you can't ask for more than that."

"Come," says the rabbi, "come look at the *mekhitza*. It's so modest, so neat. It's just right and we'll have a minyan and the Orthodox won't refuse to come in because there's no *mekhitza* and you won't be bothered by anybody. I fixed it just right."

Arnold watches us as we descend the stairs to the little prayer room.

"Inspecting the playing field?" he asks.

The rabbi opens the door to this small room, the center of such dispute. The sixth or seventh *mekhitza* is up, cut neatly, giving lots of room around the bench, and it isn't hanging from shower hooks, so no one can move it over my face.

"Fred stood right here to make sure it was right and the right distance and nobody should bother you," says the rabbi. "The main thing is, come for the sake of your father, say his kaddish, and leave, and no one will disturb you, I promise on my ancestors, on Jewish law, on my life."

It's all so dramatic, I'm shocked. I will report this instantly to Cigar as an additional scene.

I whisper to Bob, "Does this mean I have to go back?"

He smiles ruefully.

We eat deli, surrounded by our Hadassah friends and Doris, the profane kaddish sayer. Bob and I think how, in our world, we would not know these people, they would not be in our lives, and how dear they are now.

There is excitement. Along with the meat dishes, Leila, the officious woman who runs the kitchen, has inadvertently also heated up cheese knishes from the bar mitzvah of the past week, in order not to let them go to waste. We are eating milk and meat together! We are all *traif*, unkosher. The head of the Sisterhood, in her Germanic derby, rushes from table to table picking up the food.

How the Hadassah women laugh! They hate self-righteousness and pomposity. And they know they aren't *traif.*

New York, May

Mother calls. She reports on her health and I on the synagogue.

She tells me she's gone on a severe diet.

"I don't mind dying," she says, "it's having a lingering sickness I can't stand the thought of, so I'm taking off weight to help my heart."

"How are you doing otherwise?" I ask.

"Terribly," she says. "What do you mean, 'How am I doing?' I lost my best friend. That's how I'm doing."

The line is silent.

"Is it hard, Mom?"

"The hardest," she says. "I heard a good one today at my temple. 'Getting old is not for sissies.' "

We sort of laugh. It's too sad.

Mom asks, "What's doing in your *meshuganeh* synagogue?"

I tell her.

She says, "If they bother you, just tell them, 'Go kiss a bear under its tail.' "

New York, Sunday, May 17

Dad, I say, I've read the papers this morning. Guess what? Jesse Jackson tops the Democratic polls in the primary since Gary Hart dropped out of the race. Jackson received 17 percent.

My dad would probably have said, They won't let him have it.

All of the rabbi's friends are called. I sit behind the new *mekhitza*. Men come whom I've never seen before, the rabbi's Orthodox colleagues. They clutter and litter my bench. I now understand war. It's about space.

Two of the men sit down, look up at the *mekhitza*. Is it the sixth or seventh? I'm losing count, and they seem to have countless curtains at their disposal.

One man in the minyan shouts, "She's still visible."

A young man with a nasal voice is our reader. There is anarchy of prayer, everyone with a different trope, at a different speed. No one calls out the page, so I get lost until Fred announces that it is time for the *amidah,* the prayer said while standing, and I rise.

Behind this textured material I think of Spanish grillwork, of young women peering through it, sitting next to their duennas. I think of Moroccan latticework with the women in chadors peeking through.

"Raise it, raise it higher," calls a remarkably homely man about the curtain. "We can still see her face."

You're no treat for me either, Buster.

The services end. I rise to leave. I know the rabbi has been trying to convince his Orthodox friends to join the minyan, and he has succeeded. He takes my hand.

"It was so peaceful, no nice, so calm, as it should be."

I smile, nod at Fred, who is also pleased that it went well, and I leave and come home, lie down on the bed, and stare at the ceiling.

⟨⟩

New York, Tuesday, May 19– Wednesday, May 20

My sexton, my beloved shammes, has passed away.

He was the one who did me the honor of expressing impatience, annoyance, outrage at my limited learning, at my slowness of recitation.

At the same time, he called the page, pointed out the passage, stayed with me until I read or said it. Then he would relax, pat my shoulder, chortle, tell a story.

I see my grocer and inform him about the death of the shammes and that the synagogue is going to have a service around the coffin.

"It's not allowed," says the grocer quietly. "You can't have a body in the shul."

"Only in the vestibule," the rabbi assures him.

"It's *traif*, it's filth," Rabbi Ornstein shouts. "A body in the synagogue. The soul flies right out of the body, and you bring that empty casing into a place of worship!"

Joshua, Gray Braid, Schlomo, and another new devotee, Fat Retarded, cannot dissuade the rabbi.

At noon the limousine parks in front of *Beit Hatikva*.

We gather in front, his old friends, the Professor and the rabbi, his critics like the Holy Trio, and his new acquaintances, like the actor and me. Ralph has come by to pay his respects.

The coffin is a smooth, plain box that the elderly men, slipping and straining, carry through the door of the synagogue into the vestibule.

"We bring something sacred into the synagogue," says the rabbi. "The sexton was such a part of the shul for forty years that he had to be here so the walls could also weep."

In his sweet voice, with the rabbinical tremor, he sings *El Molay Rachamim,* God Full of Mercy.

It is the mothering aspect of God, the female aspect that is called upon in this great prayer of sorrow, read at every funeral. Why do they want this aspect in prayer and not the female in person?

I make this song into my own:

> May you find rest
> May you be blessed
> May you nestle
> Under the wings of the Shekhinah
> Under her sheltering wings.
>
> May you find perfect rest
> May you be blessed
> May you nestle
> Under the wings of the mothering God
> Under her sheltering wings.

The rabbi reads the sexton's favorite psalm, Psalm 16:

> . . . I have set the Lord always before me:
> Because he is at my right hand, I shall not be
>   moved:
> Therefore my heart is glad and my glory re-
>   joiceth. . . .

I had heard the rabbi tease the shammes about this psalm.

"Shammes, you like this psalm so much that you read it at every funeral."

"That's right," said my sexton.

"You want to do what's fair, don't you?"

"Sure."

"You get a hundred bucks a funeral. Give King David ten bucks, ten percent commission."

The coffin is carried out, and some of us walk in the street behind the funeral car for a block.

Little Tsibble comes from nowhere after a long absence. He runs after the coffin shouting, "Wait for me! Wait for me!"

Who will kid Tsibble about the schnapps, point out the place when he comes in late, get his tallis from the cabinet?

"Come, Old Onion," says Arnold, "let's go get some breakfast." He puts his arm around Tsibble. "An onion roll for an old onion? Cream cheese? The works?"

"Schnapps?" asks Tsibble.

"At 8 A.M. schnapps is hard to find," says Arnold, "Old Scallion, Old Leek, Old Garlic Bud."

Tsibble giggles as they go off.

Rodney, the ninety-seven-year-old, who has been acting as substitute shammes, is also stunned.

Fred says, "Look, Rodney, in the paper today, a birthday party for a guy lived to 105."

"Let me see," says Rodney. "I'll beat him."

But today Rodney can't find his hat, can't find his cane, can't find his coat.

"I didn't sleep all the night," he said, "knowing that the reb also didn't sleep."

"Oh, no, Rodney," says the joker, "I got news for you. He's the shammes for the Big Shul in the Sky."

Rodney is not convinced. "I know him twenty years," he says, "and now what am I going to do?"

He stands there so frail.

"You're going to have coffee," says Fred. "That's what you're going to do. You're going to join us for coffee."

"A quarter cup," says Rodney.

"A corn muffin, Rodney?" asks Fred.

"No," smiles Rodney toothlessly. "I got to keep my girlish figure."

Tsibble and Rodney aren't the only ones who will miss the shammes.

Leila, the buxom, officious woman who runs the kitchen, says, "I saw him every day for thirty years, and I'll see him for another thirty years. He died like a hero, making a fist."

I ask the rabbi what she meant about the fist.

"In the hospital the nurse asked him how he was doing," says the rabbi, "and he made a fist. He'll beat it. He'll get through."

Other women, my Hadassah friends, tell me about the sexton dressing up in a pink shirt and snazzy jacket and going to the Catskills, to a hotel, dancing.

"He couldn't walk so good at the end," says Fran, "but he could dance."

"He'd come in and whisper a little off-color story to us," laughs Sarah. "I remember one: A man comes home unexpectedly early and finds his best friend in bed with his wife. 'Irving,' he says, 'I've got to *shtup* her but you don't.'"

I wince. Then I remember the rabbi speaking of the shammes's life, the shrewish wife who yelled at him whenever the rabbi drove him home after his synagogue duties, "You're home already. I thought you went out on a vacation!"

"I've had four different lives," the shammes once told me. "I was in the garment business, and another work, and even a taxi driver for years with my own medallion cab. I'm a newcomer to this shammes business, only forty years."

The sexton's real life was in the society that surrounded prayer. And laughter. I will remember his singing a *hallel*, a prayer of praise, marching down the main aisle of the sanctuary, moving his arms sturdily, and with his loud, gruff voice shouting, "Hallelujah! Hallelujah!"

I never saw his wife. I wonder if she ever came to the synagogue during those forty years.

The coffin has been driven to the cemetery. The Trio, the Mafia of the *Mekhitza*, did not want to accompany the funeral procession.

Outside *Beit Hatikva* is a pail of water and a paper cup.

Leila says, "When you are in the presence of death, you must wash yourself."

I pour water from one hand to the other with the paper cup.

Leila says, "Not that way. Hold your fingers open. Pour the water all over them. You have so much to learn!"

Admittedly, but from this yelling woman and this difficult place?

₪

New York, May

Dad, news item. President Reagan told reporters he initiated the plan to use private money to aid Nicaraguan rebels.

Maybe Dad would have said, He'll get away with it. He's untouchable.

I tell the rabbi I'll be gone over the Memorial Day weekend.

"Where to?" he asks.

I make the mistake of telling him, "Face of Fire."

"Who will be there?"

"Women. Women rabbis, poets, professors."

"Just women?"

"Women."

"What do women have to say to each other?"

Upstate New York, Wednesday, May 27–Sunday, May 31

This is a group of about twenty-five Jewish feminists: rabbis, rabbis-in-training, theologians, scholars, professors, anthropologists, ritualists, community workers, and therapists, as well as a poet and novelist. The group has been meeting for over a decade at a retreat run by Catholic lay workers, women who are activists in the world and meditative at home.

It is a sacred time for the congregants. One does not come late, leave early, or miss going more than two years. Even amidst unorthodoxy there is conformity.

In the greenery of the setting and the calm presence of our hosts we hold our sessions.

Bruchot HaBa-ot, Welcome, feminine plural, for our arrival.

The first evening we sit in a circle in the living room of this pleasant frame house. Our hosts have placed flowers in vases, cleaned our bedrooms, prepared delicious vegetarian meals for us.

We go around the room and tell what has happened

to each of us and those close to us during the past year.

Our rabbis and cantors have had a hard time.

In California, a friend was fired. She is the composer of much of the joyous liturgy sung at Reform synagogues and meetings around the country. Her rabbi told the board, "It's either she or I." And he was the senior rabbi.

Another, an erudite assistant rabbi, also has a senior rabbi who insults her in every way possible. He forgets her name. He publicly corrects her. It enrages him that the congregation loves her.

In Philadelphia, the woman rabbi of a temple is beset by her male cantor.

"His voice fills the hall," she says, "whether he's singing or just announcing his presence. He can't stand my being there."

In Philadelphia, there was also the "trial" of one of our members, a brilliant rabbinical student, at the seminary. She was brought up on charges of heresy.

"I faced a tribunal," she said, "a long table of seventeen rabbis, questioning my beliefs and practices. Did I make images? Believe in a goddess?"

I had read about this trial and how, afterward, one of the rabbis shook his head in accusation, "She is very, very feminist."

I wondered how many of their students would have been on trial for being "very, very masculinist."

We breakfast, sing, study, bike, hike, dine, speak of spirituality and self-esteem. The days pass. When we leave, we hug our women hosts who live their activism and pacifism.

I return to the land of veils.

New York, June

News item: Guess what the word was that won the spelling bee, Dad? *Staphylococci.*

He would then spell it out for me correctly.

Upon my return the rabbi asks what I learned at my conference.

"It was private," I tell him.

"That's not right," he says. "Knowledge has to be shared. I was at a gathering and it happened some young women, rabbinical students, were also there, and I heard them talking Torah and arguing and explicating, and it gave me great pleasure. I told them so.

"'But you wouldn't allow us on your *bima*,' one said.

"'No,' I told her, 'but I would marry you.'"

Another *mekhitza*, the seventh, eighth? This is The Biggest *Mekhitza* in Town. How did it come to that from the smaller, more modest one that the rabbi had so carefully designed? A worshiper from the early minyan almost got poked in the eye by the curtain rod.

"It's dangerous," he raged.

Instantly, a larger, full one that hung from the ceiling was attached.

"She won't mind," says Fred. "It's got more see-through pattern."

More harm is done to me through foolishness than by malevolence.

If the world is curtained off, then why should I be behind the curtain and not in the world?

I go Wednesday to say farewell to the button man, the joker, the sports addict. I intend to daven one last kaddish.

Rodney sits directly across from me. He has become incontinent. I am jammed into a corner across from the odor of urine. I can't remove myself. The rabbi comes over to plead that I just accept it.

"You can see the *Aron HaKodesh*, the holy ark," he says. "It's just your relationship to the ark and to God."

Like a fool, I am convinced.

The new sexton is my enemy, Ornstein, busily testing the pulleys on the curtain.

New York, June

The terrible *mekhitza*.

The room is filled with new *frumies*, ultrareligious. They are elderly. Some can hardly speak. Some can hardly hear. The new sexton, Ornstein, struts around. He looks at the *mekhitza*. He had already adjusted it, pulling the cord so that it covers the bench totally. Joshua, Schlomo, and Gray Braid visibly expand.

One man, whom I've never seen before, tries to call me out into the hall. I shake my head.

"I want to talk to you," he says.

I shake my head again. I've been talked to before. He stands there insistently. I open my prayer book. The guy complains to Arnold.

"Who is he?" I ask the lawyer after services.

"A good man," say Arnold, "very active in the synagogue. He wanted to tell you why he had to hang the *mekhitza* from the ceiling."

"There are no good men," I tell Arnold.

The rabbi shows up.

"She says there are no good men left," Arnold tells the rabbi. "She wants to trade us to the bush leagues."

That guy in the hall wants to insult me and then explain why it is necessary and I should understand and accept it. It's worse than insulting.

"He's very important to us," says Arnold.

"He's a liberal," says the rabbi. "He's for mixed seating upstairs."

I like liberals less and less. I can abide righteous Orthodox less and less. Where's the space left for me—a corner of a bench, behind a full, blowing curtain?

New York, June

Rose, my friend, is mad at my involvement in the whole scene.

"Think of the energy it takes from you," she says, wearying of the story.

"It gives me good creative energy," I tell her. "Now I can only write when I'm burning."

New York, June

"How's our play going?" Mom asks over the phone.

"He wants me to keep rewriting," I tell her.

"Tell him I don't have all the time left in the world," says Mom.

"How are you feeling?"

Mom hesitates.

"No one believes me," she says. "I tell one son I hear noises, he says I'm dreaming. I tell my neighbors that someone came by in the middle of the night, they look at me like I'm crazy. I'm being invaded, I tell you."

"By whom?" I ask.

"Attacked!" she says.

"Who's attacking you?"

"A daughter also questions me," she says and hangs up.

I phone my brother in Irvine.

"She hears horses on the roof, people trying to jimmy her locks, neighbors and their relatives peering through her windows. She's put up sheets against her curtains. It's always nighttime in there."

Is that what death is? Nighttime?

New York, June

On the way to shul I walk along Sixth Avenue. A group of homeless men is standing and talking.

The tallest, an African American, tells them, "I was the only one of my family to graduate from high school. It was a good education."

At the newsstand on the corner of Sixth Avenue, owned by an Indian family, a homeless Caucasian man has picked up a paper and is reading. The shop owner hurries out to take it from his hand.

"I only wanted to know what was in the headlines," he said. "I want to be educated."

Today at House of Hope a Jewish bag man showed up. He arrived in his layers of clothing, his 1950s large brimmed fedora, carrying his dirty raincoat, all bundled up, and it is in the nineties today.

The man wears a tallis and sits quietly for the service. There is a nice *kiddish* after and he eats heartily. I leave before the others.

I hear him calling me down the street.

"Can you lend me a dollar? I asked the rabbi and he gave me a token. I'm ashamed to go back in and ask again."

But I had put my dollar into Rodney's *pushke*.

"I'm sorry," I say.

Isn't this man worthy of *tzedakah,* of charity, also?

"Tomorrow," I promise.

The rabbi comes out and walks me down the street, and we discuss the new member of the minyan.

"I told him," says the rabbi, " 'There's always a place for you. You don't even have to daven. Take a load off your feet, sit, share with us.' A Jew shouldn't have to wander any longer."

New York, June

The young lawyer, head of the Ritual Committee and slated to be the next president of the synagogue, sought me out yesterday at shul.

"We're with you," he said.

Who knows what that means?

Today he phones.

"We didn't have enough time to talk yesterday," says the young lawyer.

"This isn't really a good time for me," I tell him. "I'm writing."

"I'm writing too," he says, "legal briefs, of course." He laughs a little.

I know this is going to be bad.

"People have complained that you are opening the curtains."

"There have been six or seven curtains," I say. "I'm also complaining."

"You don't want to jeopardize the gains we're trying to make for women, do you?" he asks.

"Like what, what exactly are the gains for women?"

"Like membership. It has a very good chance unless you continue to alienate us."

"They'll vote against women becoming members because I won't stand behind the *mekhitza?*" I ask.

"It would certainly influence them," he says. "And you would jeopardize the mixed seating upstairs."

"If I stood outside of the curtains?"

"Everything would be lost," he says.

"But everything is in the basement," I say. "Everything is in that little room where I am every day and where I am hidden and hidden again and rehidden from view. That's where it is, and if you forget that, there's nothing you can do for women."

"If you're not satisfied with our policy . . . ," he trails off.

I don't hang up on him. I turn the receiver down and wait until no sound comes from it before I replace it in the cradle.

I've been fired.

New York, June

I talk to everybody about the synagogue. I have no other topic. My secular friends roll their eyes. My feminist friends shake their heads. My religious friends try to think of ways for me to get an Amen, like making a recording of ten men saying kaddish and lip-synching as I read along with them!

I ask a male friend, a therapist, "What did they want from me?"

"Everything they didn't get in their lives."

"They're babies," I say. "They want me to sew on their buttons, wipe their faces, pick them up when they fall down."

"You got it," says the therapist.

"But those others, the Bad Boys?"

"They want it too," he says, "but they can't have it. They're too mad at their mamas for dying."

"What about the curtain?" I ask him.

"To hide from themselves," he says.

"But why that long haul for my father?"

"You didn't do it for your father," he informs me. "You did it for yourself."

A friend from Detroit speaks to me about the writer Joseph Campbell, author of *Hero with a Thousand Faces.*

"You're on a quest," she says. "This is a rite of passage."

Am I going into the desert, answering a call, undergoing an ordeal? Because I love and trust my longtime Detroit friend, I pick up Campbell's book. I can easily identify the monsters of the experience, the tyrants, whom Campbell describes as "self-terrorized, fear-haunted, alert at every hand to meet and battle [as a] result of uncontrollable impulses to acquisition within [them]selves."

I recognize them. But just because those guys are monsters, does that make me a hero on a quest?

New York, June

In the Writers' Room, sunlight pours through the window. I change my clothes. For two years the members of the room have seen me only in gray sweatpants and a T-shirt. I water my plant and read the newspaper.

I pay rent to sit here and read the papers and take a nap, exercise a little, stare out the window.

And then I can locate my own address inside my head.

And work.

The novel's been derailed by my father's death.

"Don't blame me!" he would have said. "The government paid you to write."

I write daily, but about my father. I fear losing him once again, his voice fading inside of me, his appearance vague and unrecognizable.

Perhaps it is childish to hold onto him so tightly. As a teenager I outgrew him, and it was disconcerting to see him looking up at me. Yet I still feel the need to have my hand held.

New York, June

"How many characters do you have in that play?" asks Mom.

"Eleven," I say, "ten men and one woman."

"Poor dear," she says to me.

"And you. How are your days?"

"Too many characters in them, people I don't know, people I was never introduced to, coming to my house all the time, day or night."

I phone my brother. "What does she mean?"

"It means she's lonely and she's making up the rest."

New York, June

This month there was the funeral of an old friend, one of the originators of the women's movement in the seventies, especially active in the field of health. She died at the age of fifty.

The pioneers, the workers of the movement, all about that age, came to bid her farewell.

Dad, all around me, worn faces, women struggling alone, largely without partners. But those of us who started in our thirties and forties are now twenty years older, and most of us have persevered.

My father would say, Dear girl, take care of yourself.

I take care of myself by taking time off from House of Hope.

New York, June

The days are longer. I sleep later. I don't need to go swimming to work off my rage. When I'm not teaching I rise, exercise, stretch, have a leisurely coffee, and head to the Writers' Room.

I hear from Fred. Will I come for the *yahrzeit* of his "lovely lady"? I also want to say a formal good-bye to my joker, button man, sports addict. I just never fully returned after I was "fired".

It turns out that this is not the correct day for the *yahrzeit*. Fred shows his certificate to the rabbi, who looks up the right time. It will be next Monday.

"Who told you it was today?" asks the rabbi.

"Leila."

"That Leila!" says the rabbi. "It would be a miracle if she got anything right."

He then proceeds to tell a story to illustrate the danger of correcting her and then receiving such wrath in return that the whole thing isn't worth it.

There was a man who met an acquaintance, and his acquaintance greeted him warmly but said, "I'm in trouble. I need a short-term loan."

"How much?" asked the old friend.

"A hundred," said the acquaintance.

The friend loaned him a hundred, "For a week or two."

In two weeks there was no attempt to return the money. They met again.

"Where's my money?" asked the loaner.

"Another week, for sure," says the debtor, "and, in the meantime, lend me another fifteen."

A loan of another fifteen was made.

"That brings it to $115 total," says the loaner.

"You can be sure I'll repay it right away," says the debtor.

Another week passes, and they meet accidentally on the street.

The debtor smiles warmly, "Just a little longer and you'll get your money. But, in the meantime, lend me another ten."

The loan is made.

"It's $125 now," says the loaner, frowning.

"Nothing to it," says the borrower, "just give me a little time."

In a little time the borrower has not repaid the debt, but he meets his benefactor.

"I promise to repay you," he says, "and, in the meantime—"

The loaner raises his hands in the air.

"Forget it!" he says. "Forget the loan altogether. You don't owe me a penny."

"So, what can I say to Leila?" asks the rabbi.

New York, Tuesday, June 8

The vote on women. Postponed.

New York, Wednesday, June 9

A.M.

Geela, of Face of Fire, has come to visit from Toronto.

She says, "I'll go to the synagogue with you if you're still going."

With Geela, of the wonderful voice and good songs and great energy, I'd go anywhere, even to the synagogue.

"You need a support person at least once a month," she says. "You shouldn't have gone into it alone."

I don't notice her taking a tallis out of the cabinet.

We can't use the prayer room with the curtain because the air conditioning has gone off, so we're moved into another room, used for *kiddish*, without separating curtains.

Geela says, "Sit down front," and we do.

She dons the tallis and rises and covers herself with it, as I have seen the men do these months.

Ornstein comes rushing over.

"This is an Orthodox synagogue," he says. "Women don't wear the tallis. Not in my house."

Geela says, "Honor the stranger. That is *halacha*, the highest law, and wearing a tallis is only *minhag*, custom, and *halacha* takes precedence."

He is livid and hovers over us.

Geela tells Ornstein, "I need this tallis for my *neshama*, my soul. I'll think about what you've told me and see how I feel about it."

Ornstein turns his back on us. Geela not only keeps on the tallis but also sings tunefully and loudly.

The rabbi, coming in late and not noticing anything, invites Geela and me to a *kiddish*. Ornstein looks as if he'd eat us for snacks.

I rush home to tell Bob, laughing all the way.

P.M.

Mary Gordon is under the weather. I go upstate by bus to visit her.

We lie on our backs on her bed reading aloud Colette's *Break of Day*.

We make a pact to write just like that.

We both feel better.

191

New York, June

For the first time in the synagogue's history, women were voted in as members. Of course, no women attended that meeting. I had a report from Arnold.

"The former president of the synagogue objected," said Arnold. He said, 'When I lived in Germany, I was a judge and I know the law, and letting women become members is against the constitution of the synagogue.'"

"When did he live in Germany," I ask, "fifty years ago?"

"Yes," said Arnold, "and I objected to withholding membership from women, so he sneered, 'Where do you practice? Some place sleazy like landlord-tenants court?' 'No,' I told him, 'small claims court.'"

So, we put in our small claim and won.

Bob has commissioned a printer to print two of his giant woodcuts, made of collaged wood pieces. In *The Rescue*, a helicopter lowers its ladder and the victim of a flood climbs up, above the waters, to the plane. In the other, a double print on two large sheets of paper set closely together, an armed man in the pilot's cabin of a TWA plane is aiming his gun at the pilot's head.

Bob, this calm, thoughtful fellow, has disaster on the mind.

He has always hand-printed his limited editions, which is slow, laborious work. Hiring a printer is a great boon to him.

New York, June

The rabbi phones us to come to services.

After services he pours his heart out.

"Do you know about that Ornstein," he says, beside himself. "He's trying to take over, and he's going to lose. He won't let himself be called Shammes. He wants to be called Rabbi. Shammes is beneath him. Our previous shammes, may he rest in peace, would ask, 'Rabbi, who should get an *aliyah,* an honor to the Torah? Who has a *yahrzeit?'*

"If I tell Ornstein, 'Choose this person and then that one,' he replies, 'I don't know. I'll see.' Ornstein wants my job!"

Well, well, well.

Long ago, my grandmother lived with us. On cold days she would ask my dad to stoke the furnace. He would put it off and put it off. But, as my grandmother would say, "When he gets cold, I get warm."

New York, June

Another call from the rabbi, this one left on the answering machine.

"Ornstein is out. Come to shul for my mother's *yahrzeit.*"

I go to services with Bob. As I enter, the curtain has been left open from the earlier morning minyan. Gray Braid runs in and quickly pulls the cord. I stay his hand.

"Only the rabbi closes the curtain," I say.

They gather, Schlomo, Joshua, and Gray Braid.

"You're going against the laws. She thinks she runs the place."

"You got it," I say. "I run the place!"

I rise. I stalk Schlomo around the room to the door. I chase the others.

"Out! Out!" I yell.

They have maddened me. Ornstein, voted out as shammes, is still here. They're in the doorway, Ornstein with his pick-up-sticks hair, Schlomo the Bushy, Joshua with his skinny arm upraised.

"You're all jerks," I yell, "and you're all fired!"

Bob shakes his head in horror. I begin to laugh.

"I will never leave," says Joshua, "and you can't make me."

I regain my senses.

Ornstein with his thick glasses, uncombed hair, unpressed pants. Joshua, posturing. Of course they can't leave. And of course I can't make them.

The former president of the synagogue, designated as "a great liberal," rushes in and pulls the curtain shut over me.

Larry, the button man, says, "If I had my way, I'd sit right next to you on that bench and may the rest of them go to perdition."

"Trade 'em in," says Arnold.

The complainers are awaiting the rabbi, who comes in carrying hard-boiled eggs, challah, bagels, herring. He also has a friend to join him, a Hasid. The Hasid enters but won't put on his tallis or phylacteries, for I'm in the same room. The rabbi returns from his office sadly, having heard from the Holy Trinity.

He is weary. He had prepared such nice food, waiting until all those eggs became boiled and placing

them in the carton, and now the Trio will not partici-
pate in the kaddish or the *kiddish* in honor of his
mother.

"All of this fighting, and my mother was such a
peaceful soul," he says.

So was my father, pal. So was he.

New York, Wednesday, June 17

Dad, you'll never guess this who, what, when,
where, why.

Bernard Goetz, white, was acquitted in New York on
twelve counts, including attempted murder, in the
1984 subway shooting of four black youths. Goetz
claimed the men were trying to rob him. He was con-
victed only on illegal weapons possession.

Dad would have said, But if Goetz had been black . . .

New York, Sunday, June 21

It's Father's Day. All the family phones Bob.
I call out also to my father.
It's harder than I thought, Daddy.

New York, Thursday, June 25

Dad, I say, Pope John Paul II met with Austrian president Kurt Waldheim. Waldheim had been accused of helping in the deportation of Greek Jews to Nazi death camps.

Dad would have said, The church couldn't be too critical. Its hands are bloody also.

✿

New York, Sabbath, End of June

My last day in synagogue as we leave for the summer.

The rabbi devotes his service to the former shammes, who loved peace in the shul and goodwill among his congregants.

He is looking across the congregation at me, the disturber of peace.

Fran and Sarah sit with me, and we whisper and gossip. Doris stands at the back door to join us for *kiddish*. She goes to services elsewhere that are friendlier but comes here for a schnapps on her way home.

It is time for the march of the Torah.

The rabbi sings in his strong voice, shaking his parishioners' hands at the same time, as he marches up and down the aisle. To my surprise, he has chosen Joshua to carry the second Torah.

The rabbi stops before me, singing lustily, and, between notes, whispers, *"Teyerer Estherke,"* dear little Esther.

Joshua also stands before me insistently, facing me, offering the Torah.

I step back, but Joshua does not leave.

"Peace," he says and marches off, his yarmulke sparkling, his tallis flowing behind him.

New York, Sunday, June 28

Packing up to leave for the summer. The rabbi comes to our loft. He has a plan.

"Bob has been voted in as a member! The synagogue voted for women to be members! In September you will attend a membership meeting and your friends will be with you, Fran and Sarah and even Doris. Then you'll raise your hand and speak in a very respectful voice."

The rabbi speaks in a soft, sweet soprano to show me.

"You'll say, 'Ladies and gentlemen, this *mekhitza* does not have to be floor to ceiling to satisfy requirements. Other shuls have more modest separations. The *mekhitza* is, after all, a symbol.'"

The rabbi laughs. "Since the *mekhitza* is a symbol you could even suggest a bank of flowers. Can you live with a bank of flowers?"

"How do I know they won't be high, dense, the redwoods of California?"

The rabbi becomes happy. He begins to sing *Simha G'dola*, Happy Occasion. "It's a new song, very big with the Hasidim."

He has had his coffee, his bagel, his cream cheese, his lox, and his discussion.

"*Simha G'dola*," he sings as he awaits the elevator.

After he goes I hear his cantorial voice coming up the elevator shaft.

I quickly phone Cigar. I have another scene for the Broadway-bound play.

California, Friday, July 3

I am invited by the assistant rabbi of a large Reform temple in Hollywood to deliver the sermon.

I decide to read from this memoir-in-progress. I hear the response of the congregants as I speak and am also aware of the distracted senior rabbi in the front row, the same rabbi who has harassed my friend, his assistant rabbi, all year.

"I want to speak to you," the senior rabbi says after my speech, as I am surrounded by the members of his temple. "This is for your own good. Don't you know how to make eye contact? That's what speaking is all about."

I know what *he* is all about.

It reminds me of my dad near the end of his days.

He was getting ready to go to an adult education class taught at Leisure World through a local community college.

"What class?" I asked him.

"Public speaking," he said.

He peered at me nearsightedly through his thick glasses.

"I'm learning a new thing," he said. "Eye contact."

California, July

Bob is to have a one-man show at Merging One Gallery in Santa Monica in the fall. He is to deliver the rolled canvases and packed monoprints to the gallery on Tuesday, the 7th, his black-and-white photographs and four-inch-by-five-inch color transparencies. He selects what is to be framed in California at Aesthetic Frame Design.

Both coasts will now hear the sound of crashing planes.

California, Saturday, July 11

Dad, I say, the where of it is Washington, D.C. The who is Lieutenant Colonel Oliver North, who had four days of testimony about his involvement in the secret sales of arms to Iran and the diversion of funds to Nicaraguan rebels, directed by his office inside the White House.

North was characterized as "cocky and assured."

Dad might have said, Sometimes I'm glad I passed on.

California, Sunday, July 12

THE UNVEILING

Within a year, and sometimes at the end of the year, the tombstone is erected. It is called the unveiling, when the covering is removed, revealing the marble, the incised name. In our case, the granite is flat on the ground, lying heavily on my dad.

We, our family and cousins who live in the Valley, stand around the tombstone.

One shy cousin steps forward and says, "Uncle Benny was always there for me."

One group of older relatives calls my father Benny, a name he changed when he graduated from high school to Paul, more American and sophisticated.

I am surprised, as I see that mound and hold my mother's hand, that I have a fleeting memory of anger, of impatience on the part of my father.

I feel hurt by a remark I can't hear.

The unveiling ends in brunch at a deli in the Valley.

Stonington, Maine, August

We have come to Maine for years. Bob was asked, back in the sixties, to teach at Haystack Mountain School of Arts on Sunshine, an island connected by causeway to our Deer Isle.

Every August for years we drove from the Midwest to the strange land of moss green, which is misty in the frequent rain, a country of dark fir or light pine, of cormorants and seagulls, a chiaroscuro of color. Now we take the long twelve-hour drive up from Manhattan.

The waters of our bay are icy from the Arctic current.

Maine is cold in the morning, cold at night, and sun heated in the day. The leading craftspeople of the world, masters sharing their techniques, come to teach at Haystack.

We have gone there for years, having lived in cabins without water, using the outhouse. We have lived in meadows; we have lived overlooking the bay, where the light on the water was so brilliant we would wear sunglasses when gazing out the window.

Our family has dispersed, and for a decade or more Bob and I have come alone to a farmhouse in the fishing village of Stonington.

But neither on nor off the island is there a minyan.

I rise in my workroom and privately say the kaddish.

I don't hear objections from my father.

But neither do I hear an Ah-main.

Maine, Saturday, August 25

Dad, I say, a bull market on Wall Street, active trading, new Dow Jones highs, climbed twenty-five points, closing at 2,722.

My dad would have said, If it helps you, I'm glad. Otherwise, Wall Street doesn't interest me.

There is much to interest us on the island and off-island.

We have dinner with the fine artist Katherine Porter and see her new work in her studio in Harborside. We go to concerts at Kneisel Hall on the mainland in the elegant town of Blue Hill.

The Surrey People's Opera in the town of Surrey puts on *Madame Butterfly.* The singers are the local sawyer, receptionist, veterinarian, diner owner. The singing soars in the barn.

ℵ

Maine, Saturday, August 22

This is the Down East Yiddish Yodel at Joan and Bernie Weinstein's. Signs are tacked onto trees of their woods, announcing, in both Yiddish and English, the grand affair. We gather from as far away as Bar Harbor to sing, in the old *mamaloshen,* the melodies of our parents. We sing the lullabies they crooned, the early labor songs, and we end with the resistance songs of the Holocaust. That was the end of the language.

For a moment we are children again on our mothers' laps. And our children look on, foreigners to their grandparents' tongue.

ℵ

Maine, Wednesday, August 26

We go whale watching with the writer Tish O'Dowd Ezekiel. We go to Northwest Harbor, near Bar Harbor, for the boat that will take us some hours out into the ocean. This boat company is run by an ecological group that tracks whales and is determined to save the finback.

Suddenly the captain shouts, "Thar she blows!" and water spouts high into the air, and a moment later the finback emerges near the boat and then submerges. We watch this twice, holding our breath. We have seen the ancient leviathan.

We live downstairs from a lobsterman, and the grandson of the farmhouse does his own lobstering. That salty smell of shellfish is in the air. The clams, the scallops, the mussels are the great food of Fisherman's Friend in Stonington.

But, alas, Bob and I do not eat that which is without scales.

Maine is a hard place to obey the strictures of diet.

Soon we will return to the city, away from the bay, the birds, the town with one main street, but the leviathan still emerges from the waters of our dreams.

New York, September

My classes in Westchester begin, as well as Bob's at The Cooper Union.

But our minds are on his coming show.

We fly to Los Angeles on September 9. Friday, September 11, is the opening.

All of our children come, the one from New York, the three from the Bay Area—San Francisco, Berkeley, and Oakland. Sari has gone scrounging to all the Salvation Army stores and has costumed herself in an old-fashioned airline stewardess's uniform, with perky hat.

She greets the gallery-goers smilingly, "Won't you come on board?"

Nahama has recorded a tape of safety instructions we found in a booklet for flight attendants. Instructions fill the air as the gallery-goers stand before the figures and planes in danger.

Adam, one of our sons, has begun drawing and looks with pleasure at the work on the wall. He is joined by one of Bob's students from the sixties, an artist who helped found the Pop Art movement, painting giant dollar and five-dollar bills called *Big G from D.C.* and *Winkin' Lincoln*. The artist still supports himself through those early historic paintings.

Other artists, June Wayne and Ruth Weisberg, give Bob a dessert party for collectors afterward.

New York, September

Every weekday during the week before Rosh Hashanah, the High Holy Days, the rabbi blows the shofar, the ram's horn.

The crazies aren't there; the curtain is open.

"She's back!" old Rafe says excitedly. "The lady's back."

"She's not a lady," says my grocer. "She's a doctor."

The rabbi points to the reader, a teacher, someone I scarcely know.

"He was there for you. He pleaded your cause," says the rabbi. "We liberals got to stick together."

After, the "boys" take me out for coffee and a croissant. We go to Sugar Craze and I have the croissant, but the rabbi stops at a supermarket to get his own sweet, an "Entenmann" with the IU, kosher stamp.

"What money these *mashgiachs*, kosher stampers, make!" the rabbi exclaims. "Entenmann's business improved 30 percent after its stamp, and that *mashgiach* must have made for himself half a mil. The *mashgiach* for Hebrew National, a cool mil for himself for sure."

He reflects on how he could have been wealthy and not subjected to the minyan struggle and synagogue politics. Fred looks at his friend sympathetically.

"Rabbi," says Fred, "tell her what happened this summer. How lucky she was to be away."

The rabbi tells me that during our summer absence one hundred members of the congregation at a Sabbath *kiddish* came down with salmonella from the egg salad that Leila put out.

"I myself was sick for ten days," the rabbi says.

"Did you get rid of Leila?" I ask.

He shakes his head. "She runs the place," he confesses.

Later, Bob calls it "a mom-and-pop shul."

New York, September

Dad, I report, Pope John Paul II was in Detroit.

My old stomping grounds, Dad would have said.

It was reported that he squelched the cries of the Roman Catholic bishops for freedom of speech by insisting dissent is incompatible with Catholicism.

It's his candy store, my father would have said.

Also, Dad, the *New York Times*/CBS poll of the lay public questioned people on papal infallibility, on divorce, abortion, birth control, homosexuality, celibacy for priests, and ordination of women, and the majority disapproved papal infallibility and approved divorce, abortion, birth control, the rights of homosexuals, the need not to insist on celibacy of priests, and the ordination of women.

Dad would have said, It won't do them any good.

Dad, I would ask, How can you say that?

I've become more fatalistic since I died.

New York, Sabbath, September 18

Seated in the middle of the main sanctuary, greeted by good friends.

Fred is so pleased we're here. Rafe, the old man who said he made Fred a good Jew, comes over and says I'll be meeting his family Rosh Hashanah.

"You'll meet my son who went to college with Mayor Koch. You'll meet my son who got a divorce. You'll meet my granddaughters, one went to Boston U and the other to medical school. You'll meet . . . "

Rafe has a good joke. He speaks in his hoarse voice:

There was a poor pious man and a rich man who never passed through the doors of the synagogue. The rich man got richer and richer, and the poor man even more of a *kabtzen*, pauper.

So the poor man raised his voice to heaven.

"Oh God, why is my neighbor who never goes to shul so rich, and I who go every day to services am only getting poorer?" There is a noise in the sky and God's voice comes down:

"He doesn't bother me, and you noogy me all the time."

The rabbi began his sermon today: "I'm going to say a few words before I speak."

Bob grins, "We're back."

⧉

New York, Sunday, September 20

This morning was the unveiling of the tombstone of Martin Abzug, Bella's husband.

A small crowd gathered at the cemetery, Bella, bent over with the year of sorrow, and her daughters, Eve and Liz, one at each elbow.

Rubbing Bella's back was Shirley MacLaine. Gloria Steinem shivered in the cold.

Bella's rabbi had known the Abzugs since Bella taught Sunday school for him forty years ago.

He said:

> We read, at this time, of Moshe, Moses, being taken by God, and so our Moshe, our Martin, has been kissed and taken too.
>
> I will tell you that Martin's words are all around us.
>
> At Yom Kippur we speak of the martyrs of the Roman occupation. One rabbi was rolled in the *Sefer Torah*, the Book of the Torah, and set aflame. As his soul departed, a Jew cried out, "What do you see, Rabbi?" Before he expired, the rabbi answered, "The Torah is in flames, but the letters are dancing in the air."

"That's it! That's it!" cried Shirley MacLaine.

Something about that mysticism touched her, perhaps the lively letters dancing in the ether.

Despite sorrow there was a big brunch at Bella's. Her sister Helene came in bearing a noodle kugel that she baked before going to the cemetery. On end tables, on the mantel, everywhere are Martin and Bella. He is still in the apartment, his words in the air.

New York, October

"How is Mom?" I ask my brother Jay.

"Fading away," he says. "She doesn't eat. She has nobody to eat with so she has no appetite."

"How are you, Mom?" I phone her.

"All of my dresses are hanging in the closet," she says, "from every stage of my life, from sizes 12 to 42. I wish your dad could have seen how slender I've become, just the way I was when I was a bride."

New York, October

Cigar and I go out to dinner. He hands me an envelope containing many single-spaced sheets of his criticism.

"We'll get there yet," he says, hitting the envelope on the tablecloth. "Just pay attention and do what I wrote."

New York, October

The week of Sukkoth, celebration of the harvest. The rabbi and the men have gone to Williamsburg or to the lower East Side to buy the holiday greenery. The rabbi sings the song of harvest, shaking the palms, the fruit in the directions of the four corners of the earth, singing this curious Hasidic melody.

There is a parade of men carrying the palms aloft, singing. They wave branches in the air, step-dancing, Fred, Larry, Arnold, Gray Braid, Joshua, Schlomo, and Ornstein.

With their steps, with their gourd and leaves, objects of nature, the procession becomes very like the dance of American Indians.

I am, as always, an observer.

However, I had the pleasure of going into the *sukkah*, the roofless hut built on the synagogue court, and of holding the *esrog* and *lulov*, the tied-together palms and tropical fronds in one hand and a citrus fruit in the other and shaking them. I really got into it.

"They're not marimbas," laughed the *gabbai*.

Cincinnati, Ohio, Saturday, October 10–Sunday, October 11

Mary Gordon and I took a taxi to LaGuardia for the Womenchurch conference in Cincinnati. Here there are five thousand Catholic women and me. Our panel is called "On Feminist Literature from Women's Religious Experience."

The Catholic women eagerly anticipate Mary's reading.

"If you read first, Mary," I tell her, "they'll all rush out when it's my turn. You're their hero, their voice."

They are disappointed when I begin, looking at their watches, even interrupting my reading to ask how long I'll be on.

But, as I read from the novel-in-progress, *The Repair Shop*, about a little woman rabbi, they begin to laugh and listen attentively, and afterward they applaud and gather around me.

Mary begins by first informing her audience that she objects to being a metaphor, a symbol for them.

"I have a right to be a private self," she says.

A nun raises her hand. "We cannot allow you to be private. We need you and honor you for your outspokenness."

Then Mary says to the women:

The church has a grievous sin upon its conscience for which it must atone, the sin of not acknowledging our complicity in the Holocaust, in not saving the Jews. Now, the pope is going to beatify Edith Stein (a Jew who converted and took the veil.) She was hunted down by the Germans not as a Catholic but as a Jew and sent to the gas chambers. She is not a Christian martyr. The pope receives Kurt Waldheim, calling him a man of peace, and, despite outcries against this visit, the pope plans yet another return visit to Austria. We must atone for these sins of silence and complicity.

Then Mary reads the perfect title story from her collection, *Temporary Shelter*.

I hold out my arms to receive her.

"Weren't we cute?" asks Mary. "Should we go on the road together?"

The meeting of Womenchurch ends with the thousands of women parading in downtown Cincinnati.

And I wonder what it would be like to be of a religious persuasion in the land that's 58 million strong, to cast a long shadow as you walk, to have that firm step of majority, and, in that way, to be unlike the six million nervously hoppy, noisy Jews.

New York, October

We have a terrible time getting a minyan. They find a diminutive man who has only one sentence in his vocabulary, "Got a cigarette?"

"Yes," says the rabbi and entices him, with a cigarette, to be our tenth man.

He comes into the prayer room smoking.

"No cigarette," says Rodney severely.

The guy goes outside. No tenth man.

"Come in!" they call.

He returns with his cigarette.

"No smoking," says Rodney.

The man rushes out again.

Arnold begins to laugh. Fred and Larry join in and laugh until tears come.

I, who never smoke, wait an hour until a tenth man shows up.

P.M.

The rabbi has invited Bob to a Kabbalah class. Bob leaves because the men and women are separated.

The rabbi takes Bob by the arm and says to him, "If only your wife would put principle aside. It's just a matter of mourning her father."

Bob said, "But she is a woman of principle. She could never put it aside."

I'll place those words in a treasure box.

New York, October

Dad, I say, to keep you abreast:

October 1, dateline L.A.: Quake, 6.1 on the Richter scale.

October: The Dow soars again, 186 points.

My dad would have commented, You'll see. We'll have to pay for that one way or another.

October: Twenty million Americans underfed.

Dad would have said, I told you so. When the rich get richer, the poor get poorer. I learned this personally from Eugene V. Debs.

October 20: Market plunges 508 points, exceeding 1929 crash. Investors lose $500 billion from their portfolios.

Dad would have said, There was no reason for it to climb, so it had to plunge.

New York, November

We had an informal lesson at the synagogue.

The rabbi spoke of his mentor at his yeshiva, a learned scholar.

"Don't spend all your time reading commentaries on the Torah," the scholar told his students, "or commentaries on commentaries. You get far away from the original and forget the essence."

This could either be very wise or fundamentalist.

As I go further from my dad's life in these past nine months, I return to the memories of childhood.

We are in Evansville, Dad at the Evansville newspaper.

I am about three years old. He takes me with him to cover stories, sometimes with disastrous results. He is assigned the Indianapolis Five Hundred for the sports page. We sit in press box seats. A car bursts into flames in front of us. To this day I cannot drive.

I go with him into the small city prison during visiting hours to hear a prisoner talking. The prisoner pats my head. I cannot imagine why such a kind man would be in jail.

A famous evangelist, Billy Sunday, is coming to Evansville. My dad does not have the time to cover the event and urges my mother to go and take me along.

We are in a tent with a sawdust trail when the preacher yells, "If you want to beat the devil, hit the sawdust trail."

He picks up a chair, like the lion tamer at the circus. "I see old Satan now. I'm gonna whip him. Who's gonna help me fight Satan?"

I run down the aisle, my mother after me. Kicking and screaming, I feel her pull me back by the coat.

I seem to have been a kicker and screamer and, by five, a biter as well.

"Neighbors used to call the Humane Society," said my dad. "They thought you were an animal."

I imagine Dad is telling me the truth.

"And a screamer during your adolescence," says Mom, "especially in front of the neighbors."

Why did I kick and scream, bite and yell as I grew up? Was there nobody paying any attention? Was there really no interest in this skinny girl with shrieky voice and springy, undisciplined hair?

I remember my father during family quarrels. My voice would rise uncontrollably, and he would lift the newspaper before his face and lose himself in the world of printed columns.

Or my dad being so tired, working days at one job and freelancing nights at another newspaper, that his temper frayed. I was in intermediate and high school, and it was during those years that I would get shoved away from him, slapped in the face, pushed, even pushed down a flight of stairs.

He was no saint in the making in these memories that come unbidden.

I remember him impatient with his children, with me for not conforming, with a brother for not growing tall enough, with another for not learning fast enough or marrying young enough.

Nothing quite measured up: not height, not grades. He was a bit Napoleonic in my childhood. He even rubbed his sore stomach, which eventually proved to be ulcerated.

Then there was his not listening. I too had stories, not front page, not feature column, but I had my child's garden of verses, small accomplishments or failures that seemed to me to loom large.

I wanted to talk, to tell. But the newspaper went up before his eyes and did not lower until I stopped.

What is this slew of memories?

And why now, when I am almost finished with kaddish and my father has just about been beatified?

Maybe I thought if I sang the prayer over and over that he would listen, he would hear, lower his newspaper, and say, "Well done, Daughter," or even, "Forget about the news. Let me hear what's new with you."

❧

New York, November

Dad, an investigative committee has described President Reagan as having "ultimate responsibility" for Iran-Contra as well as for "pervasive dishonesty in his administration" and "disarray at the highest levels."

Dad would have said, Let me know when they put him inside and turn the key on the cell door. I could wait 'til eternity for that.

❧

New York, Tuesday, December 1

I finish Draft 3 of *Half-a-Man*, the play based upon these months in *Beit Hatikva*.

I meet with the stockbroker.

"I need to workshop it," I say. "I have to hear it. You know everybody. Can you contact somebody?"

"It isn't a play yet," he says, flicking the ash off his cigar. "It has a play within it."

As usual, more rewrites and no assurance of anything at the end.

It's funny, but the hardest character to portray in the play is the woman saying kaddish. It's not clear why she's there.

New York, Tuesday, December 1

"Mom," I phone, "I'm having trouble with the play."

"You mean, I shopped for nothing?" she asks. "I don't believe it. Fix it and let me know when to get my hair done."

📾

New York, Friday, December 4

This is my last time in the prayer room and, tomorrow, my last Sabbath as a mourner. It seems unaccountably quick.

But the rabbi never lets go. He told me to come morning and evening, for he will do a *molay, El Molay Rachamim,* at *maariv,* evening prayer. And that will be the last time the name of Paltiel ben Yaakov will be uttered publicly in the synagogue.

I had a little *kiddish* for my daily buddies this morning: loyal Fred, Arnold, steady Larry the button man, and others. They smiled at the bialys and variety of bagels: onion rolls, sesame seeds, the salt, cinnamon, plain. They licked their fingers over the herring. They spread the cream cheese.

Suddenly, Ornstein appeared. I had risen, like a good hostess, to refill someone's coffee. Ornstein sat himself down in my chair, drank my coffee already prepared with milk, ate my spread bagel. Then he held out his hand.

"May your father's memory be blessed," he said.

"Her father would have been proud of her," said Fred, the joker, and the button man and the lawyer and Rafe and Rodney and my rabbi.

That's all I wanted to hear this past year, guys.

New York, Sunday, December 13

Dad, Ivan Boesky was sentenced to three years for trading stocks with inside information.

Dad would have known about Boesky.

He's from a Detroit family, Dad would have remembered, that had a big deli, first on Twelfth Street and then on Dexter Boulevard. The Purple Gang used to hang out there. Ivan changed the pronunciation of his name from Bō-esky to Bō-sky to leave Detroit behind.

New York, Monday, December 21

More news, Dad.

I didn't expect to hear from you this month, my dad would have said. I'm on my own.

December 21: The Howard Beach trial. Three white teenagers are found guilty of manslaughter in the death of a black man. They chased Michael Griffith into the path of an oncoming car on an expressway.

My dad might have said, That's enough news to last me.

New York, Friday, December 25

Dad, I say.

You're sounding fainter, Esther.

This is news from Israel. One thousand Palestinians are in jail on Christmas for protesting on the West Bank and Gaza. There is a general strike that has also spread to the Israeli Arabs.

No more, Esther. It's coming to an end for me, Esther.

And in Jerusalem the strikes last longer. More people are involved and they're not afraid to confront the army. They say they're in despair with nothing to lose.

Good-bye, Esther. It's been nice knowing you.

New York, New Year's Day, 1988

Mom phones to wish us Happy New Year.

"I feel Dad is leaving," she says. "Do you remember what happened that night during *shivah?*"

"Yes," I say.

We don't talk about it. We just remember a year ago.

Nahama, my youngest daughter, slept in Mother's bed to keep her company.

"Suddenly," Nahama told me the next morning, "there was a blinding light. It woke me up. The *yahrzeit* candles for the dead were on, and I thought they had caught fire. But the light was reflected in the dresser mirror and was brilliant in the room. And then it faded.

" 'That's Dad saying good-bye,' Grandma told me."

"Kaddish is over," says my mother. "He's left us again."

▨

New York, January

I meet with the stockbroker.

"Should I enter a contest?" I ask.

"No, no," he says.

"Is there a workshop you can get me into?"

"I don't know," he says, puffing his cigar.

"What about Papp or the Arena or Mark Taper?" I ask.

"Not yet," he says.

"What about the Women's Project in town?"

"So call them."

"What about your friend, the head of the project?"

"I would have to tell her the truth. 'Listen, you're a dame and there's this dame here who wrote a play.'"

"That's no recommendation," I say heatedly.

He studies his cigar.

"To tell the truth, I can't totally support this play."

"Why? What's wrong with it?"

"Get that damned dame out of it. What's she doing in the play? She's irrelevant."

New York talk. Months of meetings. He had no contacts. He didn't have a clue about the play.

He wanted a place of safety that he could play around in.

My life in shul is like my life outside.

New York, Friday, January 15

The Jewish calendar puts the anniversary of my father's death in *Tevet*, a month before the Gregorian calendar date of January 15. I went through the ritual of lighting the *yahrzeit* candle for him the first time last month but felt that the race was not yet over. I had not crossed the finish line.

Then today I light the candle again. I feel, in the flicker of flame, how quickly my father's breath was quenched between one day and the next.

And I think of him and have finished that momentary anger of childhood memories.

My dad, I now realize, did not live out his dreams, he who was once "General Information" of Park Street School. He coauthored *The Jews Come to America*, the first such historical book, with his best friend Max Baker (New York: Bloch Publishing Company, 1932) and never published another book. He edited labor newspapers and a Jewish chronicle and worked for the mainstream press, but was he the journalist he set out to be at the University of Michigan when he worked on the *Michigan Daily*? Did he ever have choice, this child of poverty, this educated man who performed menial chores during the Depression, cleaning the chambers of judges in the City-County Building in Detroit?

He must have wished for so much more, and yet in his last years he turned to me and said, "The good thing about getting older is that the fierce winds of ambition abate."

⬧

Los Angeles, Spring 1988

Half-a-Man is given a reading at the Los Angeles Theater Works, directed by my longtime friend, the writer Hindi Brooks. The program is dedicated to our two fathers, who both died in the past year.

My mother attends, in a new dress, her hair done. She is walking slowly on my brother Jay's arm.

"How was it, Mom?" I ask.

"Realer than life," she says.

Jay helps her into his car to return her to Leisure World.

⬧

New York, New Year's Day, 1989

Mom calls again, wishing Happy New Year.

"Esther," she says, "listen to me."

"Yes, Mama."

"When I leave," she says, speaking more slowly these days, breathing heavily, "go where they honor you, and that way they'll honor me."

I don't reply.

"Do you hear me?"

"Yes, Mama."

"Promise," she says, "no curtains, no balcony, no last row."

She coughs and waits until she catches her breath.

"Get up there on the *bima*," she says, "and you'll stand there for me too."

"Don't go, Mama," I say.

"Don't be silly," she says. "We all go. Besides, Dad's waiting for me. But I want you to be a good girl and do what I tell you."

"I will," I say.

"That's my daughter," she says.

℞

Maine, August 1989

Mother died the last day of August, just after our annual island picnic at Sand Beach Farm.

Summer people and island people came together with potluck dishes of pastas, chicken, newly gathered mushrooms, green salad, fruit salad, seafood, and casseroles, placed carefully on the boulders surrounding the sand beach.

We ate as the sun set on the water, the hardier of the children wading into the chilly bay while others clambered over the rocks and explored the woods.

After the beach picnic, when the air cooled and the Maine mosquitoes threatened, we returned to the farmhouse for the desserts, mostly blueberry concoctions—pies, cobblers, and cakes—as well as apple, peach, lemon meringue pies and double chocolate cake, coffee, and end-of-the-summer talk.

The stars came out brightly, and the fishermen and parents of young children went home early to bed down.

Just after dawn the next morning, George, my upstairs neighbor, who has the telephone, came down and called my name.

There George was at the bottom of the stairs, formally dressed to make his announcement.

"Your brother is on the line. Your mother has died,"

and he hugged me before I picked up the phone to hear Jay's voice.

"She was not alone," said my brother. "A kindly attendant at the nursing home held her hand until she left us."

🍃

New York, September 1989

The rabbi and Fred pay a condolence call. The rabbi introduces us to his friend, also a rabbi.

"Even though you don't come to our synagogue for kaddish," says the rabbi, "what's your mother's Hebrew name? I'll give her a *molay*. I'll pray for her on Mondays and Thursdays when we take out the Torah."

I think of my mother's names: Bronya in Russia, Batya in Hebrew, Beatrice in America.

"Batya," I say.

"Daughter of?" asks the rabbi, writing it down.

"Daughter of Nechama—"

"Not her mother's name," says the rabbi. "Her father's name."

"Rabbi!" I say stubbornly. "She is the daughter of Nechama and Moshe."

He takes notes. Can I trust him to honor my mother and her mother?

Bob turns to the rabbi's younger friend.

"Where is your congregation?" Bob asks the visitor politely.

"I'm the rabbi of last resort," says the visitor.

My rabbi laughs as the visitor explains.

"There are several branches of Judaism," the visitor says, "Orthodox, Conservative, Reform. I'm Resort. I do holidays at resorts."

Fred turns to our rabbi.

"Tell her the news," says Fred.

"Do you want to know what happened to your enemies?" asks the rabbi.

Bob and I lean on the table.

"What?"

"Poor Joshua is in a halfway house. He had an episode but he's recovering. I visited him and told him we're eagerly awaiting his return. He always has a place with us."

A moment of great sweetness.

"Schlomo, who did so much shouting, has trouble with his throat. Bad trouble. He can't talk. Cancer."

I'm shocked.

"And Rabbi Ornstein, he hasn't been around in a long time."

"Where did he go?" I ask.

"To Orthodox hell," the rabbi laughs.

"Orthodox hell?" we ask.

"He's at a liberal synagogue with mixed seating," says the rabbi.

Then both of them look hard at me.

"What did you do?" they ask.

Glossary

aninut: The first phase of grief; the wailing time immediately after the death.

bar mitzvah: Marking a boy's thirteenth birthday with reading from the Torah and haftorah.

bima: The ritual stage in a synagogue containing the pulpit, ark, and Torah.

daven: Pray.

gabbai: Official at a synagogue.

Hadassah: An organization of Jewish women that raises funds for Israel, particularly for health projects.

haftorah: Commentary on the Torah.

kaddish: The fourth phase of grief; the eleven months from the time of death; the Mourners' Prayer; the one taking responsibility for the public grieving.

kiddish: A ceremony that sanctifies the Sabbath and holy days and consists of a blessing recited over a cup of wine or bread.

koved: Honor.

landsman: Someone from the same town, village, or area in Europe.

matzo: Unleavened bread eaten especially at Passover.

mekhitza: A partition separating men and women in the synagogue.

mezuzah: A small parchment scroll inscribed with scriptural verses and placed in a case fixed to a doorpost as a sign and reminder of faith.

minyan: The ten men required in attendance at synagogue to say the most sacred prayers.

mitzvah: Good deed.

phylacteries: Small leather boxes containing slips inscribed with scriptural passages, traditionally worn on the left arm and on the head by Jewish men during weekday morning prayers.

schlosshim: The third phase of grief; the thirty days after the death when no outside entertainment is allowed the mourner.

shammes: Sexton at a synagogue.

Shavuoth: The holiday of tabernacles.

Shema: The Jewish confession of faith, "Hear, O Israel . . . "

shivah: The second phase of grief; sitting at the designated place of mourning for a period of a week or less.

shul: Synagogue.

siddur: A Jewish prayer book containing liturgies for daily and Sabbath observances.

Sukkoth: Festival of the harvest.

tallis: Prayer shawl worn by men.

tefillin: Phylacteries.

yarmulke: A skullcap worn to respectfully cover one's head in the synagogue.